P9-CCO-184

Presented

By

The Otherwise Club

1985

LEE COUNTY LIBRARY
107 HAWKINS AVE.
SANFORD, N. C. 27330

D. V.

D. V.

BY DIANA VREELAND

EDITED BY GEORGE PLIMPTON
AND CHRISTOPHER HEMPHILL

LEE COUNTY LIBRARY
107 HAWKINS AVE.
SANFORD, N. C. 27330

ALFRED A. KNOPF
NEW YORK 1984

THIS IS A BORZOI BOOK
PUBLISHED BY
ALFRED A. KNOPF, INC.

Copyright © 1984 by Diana Vreeland
All rights reserved under International and
Pan-American Copyright Conventions. Pub-
lished in the United States by Alfred A.
Knopf, Inc., New York, and simultaneously
in Canada by Random House of Canada
Limited, Toronto. Distributed by
Random House, Inc., New York.

Library of Congress Cataloging
in Publication Data
Vreeland, Diana.
D.V.
1. Vreeland, Diana.   2. Fashion editors
—United States—Biography.   I. Plimpton,
George.   II. Hemphill, Christopher.
III. Title.   IV. Title: DV.
TT505.v74a33   1984   746.9′2′0924   [B]
83-49029   ISBN 0-394-50341-4

Manufactured in the
United States of America
First Edition

D. V.

CHAPTER ONE

I loathe nostalgia.

One night at dinner in Santo Domingo at the Oscar de la Rentas', Swifty Lazar, the literary agent, turned to me and said, "The problem with you, dollface"—that's what he always calls me—"is that your whole world is nostalgic."

"Listen, Swifty," I said, "we all have our own ways of making a living, so shut up!"

Then I punched him in the nose. He was quite startled. He picked up a china plate and put it under his dinner jacket to protect his heart. So I took a punch at the china plate!

Nostalgia—imagine! I don't believe in anything before penicillin.

I'll tell you what I *do* believe in. I believe in back plasters.

Let me describe this night in the spring of 1978.

I was dining very late at San Lorenzo's, in London, with David Bailey, the great photographer, and Jack Nicholson. Now don't you think Jack is just about the best actor we have? He's got a convincing face, and that funny flare in his nostrils, hasn't he? And there's something else about him which is something all great actors have—he's a great mimic. Have you ever seen his takeoff of Ahmet Ertegun, the Turk who runs Atlantic Records? He gets that . . . *thing*—that whirling-dervish *thing* Ahmet has. I think it's only from a takeoff that you can understand another person. Very often, you can't get it straight from the person himself.

But let me tell you about that night.

I was worrying about my darling friend Jack Nicholson, who couldn't sit down because his back was in such terrible shape.

The back, you know, is the most important part of your body. I'm never tired at the end of a day—never. It's because of the way I sit. At the Metropolitan Museum I have the same kitchen chair I used to have at *Vogue*. They sent it to me because nobody else would ever use such a hideous-looking thing in their swell offices—but it supports me at the base of my back, and that's what's important. Then, I have a little rubber cushion which gets me right at the end of my spine and keeps me straight up, up, up. Everyone who comes into my office at the Metropolitan thinks the cushion looks a bit medical—well, it *is*; you buy it at a drugstore—but for me, it means that I sit straight and high, and it's marvelous.

But to get back to that night. Jack's back was in such awful condition that he couldn't even sit down in the restaurant . . . walking around, tearing cigarettes apart . . . in *torture*. So I said, "I'm fed up with your back! You take every pill on the market but you don't do as I say. Tonight I'm fixing you up. May I take your driver?"

Of course, here's old Bailey, sitting there like a lump, saying in his *dégagé* way, "You can't get anything at this time of night, Vreeland. You're crazy. You don't know anything about this town."

I wish I'd made him a bet. I said, "I know this town better than you. I know where to go—Boots the Chemist in Piccadilly Circus. Open all night. Buy anything. Ask for it, it's yours."

So I got out onto the street alone, found Jack's car, and I said to George, his driver, "I'm fed up with Mr. Nicholson! He doesn't realize that what he has I've had many times—a bad back. He's got to break the spasm. He needs a back plaster. I want to go to Boots the Chemist in Piccadilly Circus. It still exists, doesn't it?"

"Of course it exists, madam."

So off we went in the biggest Mercedes you ever saw. But I began thinking there might be something to what old Bailey had said. Maybe Boots *is* open, but only for emergencies. So I said to the driver, "George, I'm thinking aloud . . . don't pay any attention to what I'm saying. I'm talking to myself. I do it all the time. It's my way of getting thoughts out. But I think when we get there I'd better *pretend* to be the patient . . . it'll make more of an impression on Boots the Chemist. So I'm now very ill . . . in fact, I've practically lost the use of my legs! How does that sit with you, George?"

"As you say, madam."

We arrived. Naturally, George could barely get me out of the car. We went in. George was propping me up, and I, naturally, was gripping the sides of the display cases, which were immaculate, beautifully lit, exactly as they were when I left London more than forty years ago.

In those days, people went in to Boots the Chemist at midnight for aphrodisiacs—Spanish fly, Amber Moon . . . big, very big. You may have heard of Spanish fly. You've probably never heard of Amber Moon, but it was *very* big. But that night I was not asking for Amber Moon, or even Spanish fly. I was not asking for anything except a back plaster. They put their hands under the counter and came up with one. "I'll take . . . *two*," I said. "I'm in terrible shape, as you can see." I took the plasters and got into the big Mercedes.

I got back to the restaurant, and George and I walked to the table. "Now listen, Bailey," I said, "you may have been born within the sound of Bow Bells, but I'm no Johnny-come-lately. I know my way around this town. I could have bought anything I asked for in that place."

Then I said to George—by this time I was very intimate with him—"Take Mr. Nicholson down to the Gents. You take him in, and I'll tell you exactly what to do with these back plasters."

"Oh, to hell with that!" said Jack. "You come downstairs and put the back plaster on me yourself."

How well do you know San Lorenzo's? Well, as you come in off the street, there's the Ladies and Gents. Do you think we bothered? No. Right in the hall. He took down his trousers. . . .

"Wonderful condition," I said. "I must say your chemistry is really good! Plump and pink."

I started taking the paper off the back plaster. Here was this big pink behind waiting for it, but I couldn't get the wrapping off the plaster. "You better get back into your trousers," I said, "because someone's going to come by in a few minutes and think this is a mighty queer act."

He shook his head. It didn't seem to bother him. Finally I got the paper off the back plaster and I said, "Now Jack, I'm going to put it on. When I put it on, you have to lean over and wriggle, wriggle, wriggle so it doesn't get too tight." I showed him myself. "Otherwise," I said, "you'll never move again."

By this time, we had a small audience looking in the door from across the street. I got the back plaster on all right. The warmth of it set Jack right up. He pulled his pants back on. Now, at least he could sit down. We went back upstairs. We ate. Don't ask me what time it was when we finished dinner—it was late. They were going on to some party. So we got back in the Mercedes and I found myself on the north side of Regent's Park.

"Now," I said, "you must take me home."

"Oh, c'mon, Vreeland," Bailey said—he always calls me "Vreeland," and I always call him "Bailey"—"you've been out later than this."

"I'm not going to any party," I said. "I don't want to see anyone but you. But as we're up here . . . I'd like to go to the other side of Regent's Park to my old house, on Hanover Terrace, which I haven't seen since I left England in 1937."

You can imagine how interesting this was for them. Every house on Hanover Terrace is identically the same. Mine, naturally, was different—once you got inside the door. At the end of the street was Hanover Lodge, which belonged to Lady Ribblesdale, where my great friend Alice Astor lived—that's Alice Obolensky, Alice von Hofmannsthal, et cetera, et cetera, Alice Bouverie . . . in any case, Alice Astor, the daughter of John Jacob Astor, the one who went down on the *Titanic*. That wonderful, divine woman—thank God she wasn't in the house when it got the direct hit from the bomb, because it was totally destroyed.

I got out of the car and went up to our house. I approached the door. It had belonged to Sir Edmund Gosse, who was quite a literary figure in the early part of this century and the last part of the last —you know, *Yellow Book* stuff. In half the memoirs of the period the address is 17 Hanover Terrace. We bought it from his widow in '29. The façade was *rien*, but the house was divine. Below the garden was a larder. . . .

I'm big on larders. I could take my bed and put it in a larder and sleep with the cheese and the game and the meat and the good smell of butter and earth. I'm always saying to people here in New York, or anywhere, "What's the matter with you? Everywhere there's a garden, there should be a larder. All you need is some good earth— dig into it and make a larder!" Oh, our larder used to be so attractive. . . .

Then, at the end of the garden, on the mews, was the garage, where we kept our wonderful Bugatti. We had a driver who was so young that when my two boys got chicken pox, mumps, measles, etc., he'd get them too. He'd write us letters all through the war. Sometime after we moved to New York, he went to work at Buckingham Palace and became the second driver for Princess Elizabeth. And one day he wrote me: "Now, madam, I drive Her Majesty the Queen." Isn't that a marvelous life?

Above the garage were the servants' rooms, in which I had radiators and wash basins installed, and a good bathroom—quite unnecessarily, I was told at least three times a week by the servants. They were petrified of the radiators—they were so afraid they'd burst. They never dared turn on the water in any of the bedrooms. Incredible race. They have a horror of running water. But they never left me. When we went to America, the two housemaids went to work at Buckingham Palace also, because the housekeeper knew someone in the royal household. The households of England in my day were a big part of life.

They had their own life. But we all worked together. That's why I could go to work for *Harper's Bazaar* when I left England—I knew how to work because I knew how to run a house. My God . . . the only chance in life I ever had to learn anything was those twelve years in England!

But I want to stick to that night. I approached the door. . . .

The topiary had gone. Of course, we had a topiary garden. At the top of the steps, on either side of the door, I put a topiary bear. Greenery, you know, is as much a part of England as a nose is part of a human face. Inside 17 Hanover Terrace, in front of the long French windows in the drawing room, were orange trees—I went down to Covent Garden at dawn for them—and with pots of cineraria plants in every color you can think of on the floor. The walls were painted a marvelous dull ochre I took from the face of a Chinaman on a Coromandel screen. Then there was Bristol blue chintz—you know what color Bristol blue is—and on it were bowknots and huge red roses. The windows went right down to the floor, and beyond the windows was Regent's Park with all those wonderful flowers and trees and boxes. Ducks in the morning. Then, as we'd be going to bed, which was invariably late, the lions were being fed—roaring and having their meal. Oh, wonderful to hear a lion roar in the middle of a city!

So that's where we lived. My husband was working in the Guaranty Trust. He left for work every day at quarter past eight, right on time, and beautifully dressed.

Reed took immense care with his clothes. He bought a great number of things—silk shirts, working shirts of discreet design, rows and rows of boiled shirts—in enormous quantity and of marvelous quality, bang, bang, bang. The hats! They're *so* beautiful. I've given most of them away. I had some chaps over and they wanted them. I've got five or six left—I'll give them to the Museum. But they were all measured and fitted. Beautiful felts—I mean, the felt was like satin. Lock's, St. James's Street. A paradise for men, just a *paradise*. I remember the last person who tipped his hat to me; it was so elegant and attractive. I was walking down Fifth Avenue and Ronnie Tree stepped out to the curb. He had on a bowler. If you remember his hair, it was that marvelous stiff hair that bushed up around the ears. You know how chic that is. Marvelous with a hat. Takes a special head; it has to be very stiff hair. He did it, tipped his hat, and it was so attractive. So beautiful. So memorable.

But then it all stopped, didn't it? Those robust pink English faces—well weathered and smiling—they're gone too, haven't they? The high color. They get it being out in those heavy, wet winds. Perhaps these days the chaps aren't out shooting so much. But in the early sixties the hats just died away overnight. I can remember Reed coming to say goodbye to me one morning, very early, and he didn't have a hat on. I said, "But you haven't got a hat." He was always totally dressed when he came in to say goodbye. He said, "I'm not going to wear a hat." That was that.

Back to Hanover Terrace. Inside, it was marvelous—but very ordinary, do you understand? I mean, we didn't have an extraordinary atmosphere of . . . light. Orange trees by the window, light coming through . . . a very English light.

That night, I stood at the front door and looked. The stoop was very well kept which is that English thing and which makes all the difference. But the door was painted a hideous color. When we lived there it was pickled—every surface removed and then polished. Every door inside was an Oriental red, but one didn't come *in* through a red front door. I stood in front of the door. Through the side windows there was nothing to see. It was just a blah house. But there on the door was my old door knocker, a pathetic little hand. It had been on that door since 1930, through the Blitz and that whole bloody bit. A door knocker! Ah, but it was more! I bought it in St. Malo when I was very young—and we were going to miss the boat to wherever we were going. So I said to Reed, "That little hand—I like it so much." So we knocked on the door and a woman came out and after twenty minutes —the French are very generous if you offer them money—we came away with the door knocker. It was an interesting little Victorian door knocker, no *grand'chose* about it, but ah, my God! And then I turned around, went back down the steps, got back in the car, and said to David Bailey and Jack Nicholson, "And now we are going to the party!"

CHAPTER
TWO

"Vreeland—with a V!" I say whenever I have to give my name over the telephone. "V as in 'victory'! V as in 'violent'!"

But I can remember a telephone operator saying to me when I was living in England, "No, madam—V as in 'violet.'"

I loved the put-down. She put me right back where I belonged. "Yes," I said, "you've got a *point*."

I liked the violet touch.

My sister, Alexandra, has violet eyes. She's four and a half years younger than me, so she was still a baby when my family moved from Paris to New York in 1914. I can remember she was The Most Beautiful Child in Central Park. In those days it was a very small world, and there were all sorts of little titles like that. She'd sit in her pram—she was terribly dressed up, you understand—and people would stop just to look at her. As soon as I'd see people looking, I'd run over to the pram, because I was so proud of her.

"Oh, what a beautiful child!" they'd say.

"Yes," I'd always say, "and she has *violet eyes.* . . ."

Then there was the most terrible scene between my mother and me. One day she said to me, "It's too bad that you have such a beautiful sister and that you are so extremely ugly and so terribly jealous of her. This, of course, is why you are so impossible to deal with."

It didn't offend me *that* much. I simply walked out of the room. I never bothered to explain that I loved my sister and was more proud of her than of anything in the world, that I absolutely *adored* her. . . . Parents, you know, can be *terrible*.

My mother and I were not really sympathetic. Very few daughters and mothers are. She was very good looking. I'll tell you who we are on the American side: Hoffman and Key from Baltimore. Francis Scott Key was my great-great-uncle. My mother was born Emily Key Hoffman. Her father was a man called George Hoffman. I know nothing about Baltimore; I know nothing about my background. I know that my great-grandmother and her sister had a lawsuit over a dining-room table, and the judge was so fed up—this was in Baltimore —that he had a carpenter come in, cut the table in two, and say: "You two women get out of here and stay out, each with your own slice!"

My parents met in Paris. My mother's family, though American, was always in Europe. My maiden name is Dalziel—pronounced Dee-el. Dalziel was once listed in *Reader's Digest* as one of the three most difficult names in the world to pronounce. One of the others was Cholmondeley (pronounced Chumley); I can't remember what the third was, but I'm sure it was English. Impossibly difficult language. Dalziel goes back to 834, Kenneth II of Scotland. It means in old Gaelic "I dare." That's me.

My father, Frederick Y. Dalziel, was a totally continental Englishman; he had no more to do with New York than I would with Persia or Siberia. My mother was very brunette. As brunette as I once was, but of course she was a beauty. I didn't look like her at all. She was one of the beauties of La Belle Epoque in Paris, no question about it.

I was terribly fortunate—don't think I'm not grateful—in that my parents loved us very much. They were racy, pleasure-loving, gala, good-looking Parisians who were part of the whole transition between the Edwardian era and the modern world. Money didn't seem to be of any importance to them, and they were wonderful in the way they surrounded us—not because of us, but because of the life they led—with fascinating people and events. All kinds of marvelous people came to the house, Irene and Vernon Castle. Nijinsky came with Diaghilev. He wasn't impressive, exactly, but he was there—you were aware of him. Diaghilev was very impressive. He had a streak of white hair and a streak of black hair, and he put on his hat in the most marvelous way. I remember him very clearly. But little Nijinsky was like a pet griffin. He had nothing to say. Of course, we knew we were seeing the greatest dancer in the world. We just knew it—you can't fool kids.

My nurse, though, was appalling. Naturally, nurses are always frustrated. They may love the children, but they're not *theirs*, and the time will come when they will have to leave them forever. I couldn't stand mine. She was the *worst*.

But I have to say there was one terribly attractive thing about her which I've always remembered. Her name was "Pink." I've always thought that name had great style.

Every day in Paris, except Wednesday which was her day off, Pink would take us from our house on the avenue du Bois, now avenue Foch, to the Bois de Boulogne to play. On Wednesday, my grandmother would lend us her secretary, Miss Neff, this ghastly, god-forsaken, broken-down, American old thing—but *old*—who always wore the same ancient black lace dress. On Wednesday, Miss Neff would take us to the Louvre to see the *Mona Lisa*. Always the black lace dress, the Louvre, the *Mona Lisa*. . . .

One day for the hundred-and-tenth time we were shown the *Mona Lisa*. We had to stand here and then there, *here, here,* and *here,* because, as Miss Neff used to explain to us every time, "she is always *looking* at you. . . ."

My sister and I always did as we were told, so we *did* get to know the *Mona Lisa* rather well. This particular Wednesday afternoon, we saw it from so many angles that the guard had to come and tell us to get out because we were the last people in the Louvre. I can remember our hollow little footsteps as we walked through deserted marble rooms trying to get outside. The next morning it was in all the newspapers that the *Mona Lisa* had been stolen during the night.

I think they eventually found the poor old girl in a trash-can in the dank bathroom of a poor artist, cut out of her frame and rolled up. For two years she hadn't been unrolled. Don't forget, it was the most famous painting in the world, and don't forget how small the world was in those days. It was a *total tragedy*. It was like the kidnaping of a child you love more than anything in the world.

It was a big story when they got her back, but it was a *bigger* story when she was stolen. My sister and I were the last people to see her before she disappeared. For one day we were the most famous children playing in the Bois de Boulogne. The next Wednesday, when Miss Neff was supposed to take us to the Louvre to see the *Mona Lisa*, of course it wasn't there. Do you think at that age we cared very much? No, to us it was all a great relief. We were taken instead back to the Bois, which I *much* preferred.

Actually, my dreams are in the Bois. I was brought up in a world of "great beauties," a world where lookers had something to give the world, a world where the cocottes, the women of the demi-monde, were the great personalities of Paris. They were the great hostesses, the great housekeepers, the great women of glamorous dress. They were in their own half-world and that half-world was *very* important. And the Bois was where they paraded early in the morning. That was the secret of the beauty of the demimondaines. They took the morning air. They were there at eight-thirty in the morning. Then they went back home to rest, for a massage, and to arrange the menus of the evening for their gentlemen friends. They went to bed much earlier in those days, you know . . . these midnight dinners such as we attended in the last few years are for the birds. So these demimondaines were extraordinary beauties.

Naturally, I've always been mad about clothes. You don't get born in Paris to forget about clothes *for a minute*. And what clothes I saw in the Bois! I realize now I saw the whole beginning of our century there. Everything was new.

Of course, much was the influence of Diaghilev. The flavor, the extravagance, the *allure*, the excitement, the passion, the smash, the clash, the *crash* . . . this man smashed the atom! His influence on

Paris was complete. The Edwardian era before it had been as strong as steel. It was going to stay until something else came along. Well, that something else came along and swept *everything* in its wake—including fashion, because fashion is a part of society and a part of life.

The colors! Before then, red had never been red and violet had never been violet. They were always slightly . . . grayed. But these women's clothes in the Bois were of colors as sharp as a knife: red red, *violent* violet, orange—when I say "orange" I mean *red* orange, not yellow orange—jade green and cobalt blue. And the *fabrics*—the silks, the satins, and the brocades, embroidered with seed pearls and braid, shot with silver and gold and trimmed with fur and lace—were of an Oriental *splendeur*. There's never been such luxury since. These women *looked* rich.

Their silhouettes were totally new. Almost overnight, the trussed, bustled, corseted silhouette of Victorian women disappeared. Poiret was the designer responsible for the shift in fashion—from "La Belle Epoque" with its beautiful Edwardian women with their gigantic eyes and their hard corsets. Women then had a waist and bazooms, and I suppose they had a stomach and everything else. But Poiret removed everything. The corset went. In place of curves there was a straight line. It seemed that everyone became streamlined to the ground. The naturalness of these women's bodies was what was new. But often their skirts were so tight they could hardly walk. I can remember them balancing *enormous* hats trimmed with birds of paradise, cockades, and aigrettes, walking through the Bois with tiny, mincing steps. . . .

Their *shoes* were so beautiful! Children, naturally, are terribly aware of feet. They're closer to them. I remember shoe buckles of eighteenth-century paste, which is so much more beautifully cut than rhinestones are—so much richer looking. I love decor on the foot. To this day, that's the way I like shoes.

And *horses*! The automobile was new, but these women maintained horses, and always in pairs or in tandem. In my childhood, their beauty and the beauty of the women who owned them were inseparable.

Think of the Champs-Elysées—it's still the same . . . though there are fewer trees, and they don't seem to grow as lushly as they did then. It's still so restful to the eye—its straightness and length. . . . I can remember races up the Champs-Elysées to see whose teams—a pair of grays or bays—could make it up the last hill at a trot without breaking—that was a bit of news! It was all part of the glory of these women —and of the men who kept them.

Do you know who knew all about these extraordinary women? How well do you know Maxim's? Well, as you come in off the street, naturally there's the doorman. Then there's the head *chasseur*—or there used to be. The *chasseur* was a runner. He was the one you'd ask to go out and buy three copies of *Paris-Soir* or whatever— there were always runners—and they'd be delivered to your table.

Several years after World War II, an important *chasseur* at Maxim's, a very old man, offered his *cahier*—his little notebook— about these demimondaines of the Belle Epoque—to *Harper's Bazaar*. Don't ask me how it fell into our laps. But *Harper's Bazaar* had a great name in Paris in those days. Also, Carmel Snow, the editor in chief, was a great personality in Paris then; everyone knew this crazy, brilliant Irishwoman. Drunk or sober, they adored her. She was always marvelously dressed. And she was often very drunk—I don't mean tipsy. She would talk absolutely brilliantly—but she couldn't get up and walk.

But that's not the point. The point is the *cahier* that Carmel passed on to me. I had it translated and published in *Harper's Bazaar*. And do you know that not one person on the magazine, and not one reader, mentioned what an extraordinary social document it was.

It was a tiny, odd-looking notebook. You know how economical the French are with paper. You and I leave the first page of a notebook blank and start on the right-hand side. This *chasseur* was a real French peasant: he started on the left, so far up that there wasn't any paper left above the first line. In this notebook was a list of all the available women of Paris, with complete descriptions—things like "mole on left hip" and *"pas tout à fait de premier ordre"* and "born in

Chaillot" and "Baronne not to know" and . . . et cetera. This little old man . . . just *think* of it: he was the only person in the world who knew that there was a girl with a mole on the left hip very much desired by the Duc de Quelque Chose at one time but who, since his passing, was not perhaps *assez connue*—and therefore should bring a big price! I mean, this was something fantastic. You couldn't make it up, because, as everyone knows, truth really is stranger than fiction.

The great ones were the English. They were marvelous. Their demands were very, very firm. The demimondaines could have as many lovers as they wanted as long as *nobody* knew it. The demimondaines had their own newspapers; they had their own hair-dressers; they had their own dressmakers. You've seen *Gigi*. They knew how to test a cigar; they knew brandy, and they knew wine; they could pick out chefs. Many of the men did not live in Paris, but they maintained great houses there. A marvelous old girl who used to work for Christian Dior told me, "And don't forget, Madame Vreeland, that we were often the front for the Englishmen who only came for the boys. The girls were the front. We ran the house; it was *apparently* for us. We'd get a pink pearl from an archduke and a gray pearl from a grand duke, and it was all very luxurious and wonderful. The gentleman had to be kept absolutely immaculate in the eyes of his friends . . . putting on a show with the new sable coats and the new pair of grays and the beautiful carriages, and the whole bit." She used to tell me a lot, because she had been so magnificently well kept herself.

In 1909 Diaghilev brought Ida Rubinstein to my parents' house on the avenue du Bois. He thought my mother had wonderful taste. It was very important to him. If my mother approved, Ida Rubinstein, a great beauty and a totally unknown dancer who was being championed by Fokine and Bakst, would play the title role in *Cléopâtre*, and Lord Guinness would help to pay for the entire season of the Ballets Russes at the Châtelet. Now Lord Guinness was one of the great keepers of Paris women. Perhaps he liked the boys as well. Therefore, to protect his reputation, so to speak . . . Ida Rubinstein would act as a kind of front.

My sister and I, you know, missed nothing. No children do—unless you keep them locked up in a padded cell. I was behind a screen. And Ida Rubinstein came in. . . .

She was all in black—a straight black coat to the ground. In those days, you kept your coat on indoors because you never knew what the temperature would be. At the bottom of the coat was a wide band of black fox to *here*; at the collar and cuffs were wide bands of black fox to *here* and *here*; and she carried an *enormous* black fox muff—it was almost like sleeves—that she put her hands in as she came in the door. Under the coat she wore high black suede Russian boots. And her *hair* was like Medusa's—these great big black curls, draped in black tulle, which kept them in place and *just* veiled her eyes. Then her *eyes*, through the veil . . . I'd never seen kohl before. If you've never seen kohl before, brother, was that a time to *see* it! These long, slow eyes—black, black, *black*—and she *moved* like a serpent. But there was no danger. She was long, lithesome, sensuous, sinuous . . . it was all line, line, *line*. She wasn't a trained dancer, but she wanted to be in the ballet. I think she came from quite a rich family in St. Petersburg—a sexy Jewish girl with quite a lot of money.

My mother was fascinated by her. She gave her approval to Diaghilev. I can remember her saying to him, "She may not be a trained dancer, but after all she has nothing to do but lie there with a look of *complete pleasure* on her face."

As you probably know, in this spectacle she was carried in on the backs of four Nubians, who naturally were dressed in solid seed pearls. She had practically no clothes on. She had one big turquoise ring on her toe . . . so pretty. There was a terrible orgy where everyone *consumed* everyone else . . . but she didn't have to do a thing.

Diaghilev was more than pleased, because he knew that the entire season at the Châtelet would be supported by Lord Guinness. Lord Guinness was also pleased as punch, because he had his front. And that's where everything happened, and 1909, that's the year it happened, and they say that's *how* it happened.

CHAPTER
THREE

In retrospect, I adore the way I was brought up. I adore the amount I knew before what I know today and I adore the way I got to know it. My experiences were so innocent and so easy and so charming. I grew up in the springtime of so many things. There was still the British Empire. I'm a product of the empire. I don't think anyone realizes what the riches were like.

I've had no formal education; I'm the first to say it. But my family did think of the most wonderful things for my sister and me to do. They sent us from Paris to London with our nurses and we sat in the bleachers and watched the coronation of George V in 1911. The excitement lasted three days and three nights, so you can imagine what I could say about *that.* You could say a child of my age wouldn't have taken it all in. But you have no idea what I *did* take in, what I did see. . . .

Everything was horses. There were skewbald horses, piebald horses, and there were tiger horses, roans, greys—those beautiful prancing animals bred in Hanover especially for the equipages, the carriages, and the liveries. Terribly big-time stuff.

Everything was a principality, you see. Don't forget how many states, for instance, there were in Germany. I can't even remember the names anymore—Hanover (they were the ones who bred the horses), Saxe-Coburg-Gotha, Saxony, Prussia, Bavaria, Württemberg, Schaumburg-Lippe. There was the King of the Belgians with all his equipage. The Kings and Princes of all those Balkans—Albania, Bulgaria, Greece, Montenegro, Serbia—with their equipages. And the Czar of all the Russias—I mean *all* the Russias—with *his* equipage. The Hungarians. The Rumanians. And the Turks. And the *Chinese.* And the *Japanese.* We really had to know our geography then and, what's more, we really did. The mélange was something so incredible. I love a mélange. That is still Europe to me—a mélange of bloods, races, chemistry. . . .

Don't forget how bizarre it all was. I mean, the King of Serbia—*that's* bizarre! And don't forget that King George and Queen Mary were Emperor and Empress of India. The maharajahs were a dime a dozen, and they put jewels on their elephants—their *elephants!* They all had elephants if they were any good! Do you realize what an elephant is today? They're even hard to find in *India.* During the coronation in London, my sister and I saw them go by like taxis on Park Avenue. Until the night was black. It was so exhausting. I was so sleepy and so *bouleversée.*

Maharajahs and maharanis, the Czar and the Czarina, the Kaiser and the Kaiserin . . . and Queen Mary and King George V! She passed by for just a few minutes, but to this day I would recognize her as I recognize you. Of course, later I lived there for many years of her reign. There was something about the way she sat and her proportions and the size of her hat which was immediately recognizable and never changed. A very, very good idea, hats—especially for queens. The toque was worn over a pompadour and fringe, giving Her Majesty *hauteur* and revealing the face. Queen Mary's hats tended to look like the head of a secretary bird, a sort of a brush of a thing; they looked as though they could be taken off and used for something—to dust the house.

Queen Mary was Edward VII's daughter-in-law, and she was an Edwardian. I'm mad about her stance—it was up, up, *up,* and so was she. The Edwardian influence in England lasted long after

Edward's death and blossomed like a cherry orchard in the best sun. Each period casts a long, long shadow. That's my period, if you really want to know. You might think it was my mother's period, but it's mine. One's period is when one is very young.

Actually, when I was brought to America from France in 1914, I didn't know any English. But what was worse, I didn't *hear* it. I was the most frustrated little girl. I was sent first to my grandmother's house in Southampton, Long Island, in the month of April (which is an odd month to go there, but never mind; it was never explained to me then, and I have no way of finding out now). Then the war broke out and we were stuck. And I still couldn't speak English.

My family moved from Long Island to a tiny little house on East Seventy-ninth Street, one door off Park Avenue. My sister had a floor with her nurse and I had a floor with my nurse. All I cared about was horses. I never had a doll. I only had horses—these little toy horses I kept in little stalls along one side of my room. I'd stroke them and talk to them in a curious language of my own. I can't remember much of it except that chickens were "uddeluddels" and elephants were "eggapatties." I talked to them all night. The awful thing was that I adored my horses so much I'd get up in the middle of the night to see that they had water; then the glue on their manes and their tails would run. The room always smelled of glue, which is like dead fish.

My grandmother had a huge farm horse in the country outside of Katonah, New York, who wasn't used a great deal. He just stood in his stall. After lunch I'd run off, get on the horse. I had to use steps because he was *enormous*, and I'd sit there all afternoon, perfectly happy. It would get hot, the flies would buzz . . . occasionally he'd swat his tail because the flies were bothering him, and I'd just sit there. That's all I wanted—just to be with the *steam* and the *smell* of that divine horse. Horses smell much better than people—I can tell you *that*.

I was almost intuitive about horses. I can remember standing on the corner of Seventy-ninth Street and Park Avenue. I'd suddenly say, "Horse, horse, horse!"—and a horse would come around the corner! Naturally, my fixation was practically over by then, but I could smell the oats and the hay coming around the corner. Because there's quite a steep slope there on the corner, many horses slipped, broke their legs in the snow and ice, and had to be shot. And of course it killed me. Children, you know, are so *tragically* dramatic. The death of a horse to me was something so *terrible*—because I didn't give a *damn* about anything else. Don't forget, I still couldn't speak any intelligible language.

I certainly didn't give a damn about school. I was sent to the Brearley School. It's one time in my life I've always regretted—fighting my way through the place. . . . And those goddamn *gongs!* Everyone knew where to go when the gong went off except me, but I didn't know whom to ask. I didn't know anybody, I didn't know anything—I couldn't *speak*. By this time, stuttering had started. You see, I wasn't *allowed* to speak French. But you have to talk. You have to say, "I want some bread" or "I want some butter" or "I want to go to the . . . bathroom"—but I couldn't *say* it!

I can remember a teacher named Mrs. McKiver who always used to say, "If you can't say it, you don't know it." You can imagine what that did to me.

So this terrible stuttering began . . . several doctors were brought in. They said, "Mrs. Dalziel, either she speaks French or English, but right now she's totally confused. There's got to be a decision." English was decided on, which is why I speak such terrible French to this day.

I can remember my mother coming to Mothers' Day at the Brearley School—you can imagine how much that interested her—and I can recall exactly what she had on. She wore a *bright*-green tweed suit and a little gold-yellow Tyrolean fedora with a little black feather, gilt at the end, that was short but sharp—I'm talking *sharp*—and she was *very* made up. Well, of course, this went around school: "She's got diphtheria," or "She's dying of cholera." Naturally, I was mortified.

My father was so much easier and closer to us. He was the

most wonderful, affectionate man—six foot *six* . . . well, by God, there was an Englishman! Six foot and a half. And when he'd meet us at the train station—in those days, of course, you'd travel by train—you'd see him easily in the crowds waiting at the gate, whether it was London, Paris, or New York. He had that *thing* about him, having to do with a sense of humor, which is the most cleansing thing in the world. He was a raring, tearing beauty, who lived to the age of ninety-three with all his brains and everything . . . but he really had nothing to do with the modern world at all.

My father had the English accounts for Post and Flagg stockbrokers. I never really knew what a stockbroker did; I'm not sure I do now. He was in business after World War I, so I mean . . . where was the money? He never had any money, never made any money, never thought about money; it killed my mother, who was American, though she was very European. She saw things rather square, which most women do. You know, women *are* squares. I mean, it's very important. Women do care that their children have something to eat. Husbands aren't so concerned. Supposing you were my husband: you might well say, "Oh, I'll see you in a couple of weeks, I'm off. I don't *quite* know where I'm going."

Well, Brearley kept me for three months, and then they told my mother, "Mrs. Dalziel, she's not . . . *us!*" And I certainly wasn't. I was looking for something Brearley couldn't offer.

I discovered dancing. I was taken out of Brearley and sent to dancing school, and I *adored* it. It was the only school they could keep me in. I was with the Russians—first Michel Fokine, the only Imperial ballet master to ever leave Russia, and later with Chalif.

I did Pavlova's *Gavotte* at Carnegie Hall. In the Metropolitan Museum we have a delicious figurine by Malvina Hoffman showing Pavlova doing the *Gavotte*. I did it alone, on the great stage, but it certainly wasn't any *grand'chose*. Don't think the house got up and stormed the stage or anything—we were just the pupils of Chalif. But the *Gavotte* is so pretty. I remember coming forward in an *aigre pois* dress held out to here and a *deep* poke bonnet. I was *alone* doing this and I was terrified. I only wanted the joy of interpreting the dance

—the *Gavotte*—but realizing that I was being seen, I suffered, as only the very young can suffer, the torture of being conspicuous.

I was also taught *The Dying Swan*, which is the most extraordinary thing because of the *tremor* that goes through this creature. In the most extreme positions one leg goes out, out, *out*, and then the head comes down, down, *down*, and the body is moving, *quivering*, in a death spasm . . . oh, it's too beautiful! It's beauty that's leaving the world. . . . Of course, it was the most wonderful education for a young girl, because I had to interpret it for myself.

Someone once told me that Pavlova learned *The Dying Swan* from watching a swan die in Southampton. I've since learned that Pavlova came to the United States *after* the choreography of *The Dying Swan*. But it's a nice story, and I could very well believe it. I spent so many years of my life on that Southampton beach in the marvelous summer air. Every rainy day, when I couldn't be on the beach, I'd walk around the lake, where I used to watch the swans by the *hour*. The beauty of those swans! Of course, they're angry beasts, like peacocks; but where peacocks are common, there's nothing common about swans. The *silence* of their swimming . . . you don't hear it, but you feel it. All I'd hear would be the sound of the rain, but I'd feel that wonderful salt and brine that's as strong just inland as it is on the beach.

One day in 1917 my sister and I were playing on the beach, as usual, and then we were put to bed. During the night, there was an outbreak of infantile paralysis in Southampton. There was going to be an epidemic on the beach! So that same night we were awakened and dressed and with my mother's French maid—don't ask me why it wasn't an English-speaking nanny—motored for eight hours to Pennsylvania Station, where we were put on a train to Cody, Wyoming. Don't ask me why Cody was chosen. I suppose my mother had heard of it and it sounded remote and romantic. We didn't make it to Cody. In Butte, Montana, with a background of roaring copper mines, there was a railroad strike, so we were stuck.

Believe me, the West was still the West then. We were put to bed that night—the French maid, of course, was in hysterics in the next room, not knowing where she was or quite what had happened to her—and we sat at the window, my sister up on a pillow, and looked out onto the street. *Everyone* was drunk. The men would say "Dance, dance, dance!" and they'd shoot bullets into the ground and dance around them and then they'd say "Dance, dance, dance!" The great thing was to jump. Then they'd shoot bullets through their *hats* . . . and sometimes they'd miss. Men were falling over—*dead*.

Don't think we were frightened. It was all so totally bizarre. It was a world of which we knew nothing, so it didn't affect us *that* much. To this day, anything physical or strange . . . I can usually pass it off by saying it was a very healthy experience.

Eventually we got to Cody, where my mother joined us. We were there in the wilds with the moose and the bears and the elks and . . . my *word*! It was so *lonely*. I remember lonely men, lonely spaces . . . I couldn't stand the loneliness of those cowboys. They weren't romantic to me. They were just lonely, ordinary guys who used to sing these sad songs around the fire . . . this may not be sensitive, but it's as sensitive as *I* care to get. It wasn't big-time stuff.

But we did meet Buffalo Bill—he was a bit of all right. Cody was named after him, and if you lived in Cody you knew Colonel Cody—Buffalo Bill. He was essentially an entertainer. But what chic old Bill had! With his beard he looked like Edward VII, and he wore the fringed leather clothes that the hippies all wore in the sixties. By the time we met him, he'd already been received by European royalty and was covered in glory, fringes, gauntlets, and sombreros. To us, he was just an Edwardian gentleman who happened to be in Wyoming, just as we happened to be there.

We stayed with him long after the school year had started. He rode beautifully, and he was so sweet to us, giving us these little Indian ponies which we adored.

My mother's horse, our two ponies . . . that was all I had out West . . . and old Bill. The last time I saw him was when he came to see us off on the train that was to take us back to New York. I can remember standing with my sister at the back of the train with tears pouring down our faces, waving. . . .

I was so lonely in Wyoming. But I think when you're young you should be a lot with yourself and your sufferings. Then one day you get out where the sun shines and the rain rains and the snow snows, and it all comes together.

It all came together for me when I got back to New York. I went back to dancing school and I didn't give a *damn* about anything else. All I've ever cared about since is movement, rhythm, being in touch—and discipline. What Fokine taught.

He was a brute. He'd put you at the barre, he'd place his cane under your leg . . . and if you couldn't raise your leg high enough, then—*whack*! One day he tore my leg to ribbons—all the ligaments. It just went. I was laid up with my foot up and my leg up for eight weeks. That was nothing in *his* life. But he taught me total discipline. And it's stood me in good stead all my life—it's forever!

I'm talking about strict rules, bash on, up and away! . . . still, my dream in life is to come home and think of absolutely nothing. After all, you can't think *all* the time. If you think all the time every day of your life, you might as well kill yourself today and be happier *tomorrow*. I learned this when I was very young. When I discovered dancing, I learned to dream.

CHAPTER
FOUR

Japan! When I got to Kyoto, the eighth-century capital of Japan, it was truly a dream come true. Under the pine trees there I felt an element of the centuries as I'd never felt anywhere before in my life. Everything old there is so beautifully maintained. But there's nothing slow about Kyoto—everyone's on motorbikes wearing Saint Laurent shirts. What's extraordinary is the way everything modern fits in with everything old. It's all a matter of combining. There's no beginning or end there—only continuity.

God was fair to the Japanese. He gave them no oil, no coal, no diamonds, no gold, no natural resources—nothing! Nothing comes from the island that you can sustain a civilization on. What God gave the Japanese was a sense of style—maintained through the centuries through hard work and the disciplines of ambition.

When I saw the *meikis* carrying these beautiful umbrellas, walking over these acres of moss in the shadows of a rainy night under these beautiful willow trees with their knees just *slightly* bent . . . do you know what *meikis* are? They're the girls who are training to be geishas. You'd think that a geisha was made up like a *meiki* until you knew the difference. A geisha is very *tenderly* made up, and everything about her hair and her clothing and everything else is very exquisitely done. But everything about a *meiki* is a great exaggeration —her obi is *this* wide, her skirt is padded at the bottom with a row *this* wide, her back panel is out to *here*; she has *very* white makeup, *very* red makeup. . . .

The idea must be that you learn from the exaggeration.

This is a very serious subject with me. I've given this a lot of thought. I adore dressing and I adore making up. I adore the procedure—it's terribly invigorating, both during my getting up in the morning and during my getting ready to go out in the evening. It gives me such pleasure.

I adore artifice. I always have. I remember when I was thirteen or fourteen buying red lacquer in Chinatown for my fingernails.

"What *is* that?" my mother said. "*Where* did you get it? *Why* did you get it?"

"Because," I said, "I want to be a Chinese princess."

So I went around with these *red* red fingernails—you can imagine how big that would have gone over at the Brearley School.

Then . . . when I'd started going out a few years later, I discovered calcimine. If I was going out—and I went out almost every night—two and a half hours before my escort arrived I'd start with this huge bottle of calcimine (I forget the brand, but it was theatrical stuff)—a sponge . . . and I'd be *totally* calcimined from the waist up, out along the arms, the back, the neck, the throat, et cetera, et cetera. I had to do this alone, because my family didn't take much interest in what I was doing. Then, when my escort and I would get up to dance, he, in his black dinner jacket, would be *totally* white. I would come off on him. But he'd have to put up with it. It meant nothing to me—I looked like a lily!

On the night of my coming-out party in 1923 . . . was I calcimined *that* night! I was whiter than white. My dress was white, naturally. And then the reds were *something*. I had velvet slippers that were *lacquer* red. I carried red camellias. In those days everyone sent flowers, and I'd received something like fifty bouquets. One huge bouquet of red camellias was from a big-time show person: J. Ringling

North. "*Circus people* . . . where did you ever meet *them?*" my mother wanted to know. I told her that for some reason J. Ringling North had taken a fancy to me and sent the red camellias.

My mother disapproved. "You should know," she said, "that red camellias are what the demimondaines of the nineteenth century carried when they had their periods and thus weren't available for their man. I don't think they're quite . . . suitable."

I carried the camellias anyway. They were so beautiful. I had to assume that no one else at the party knew what my mother knew.

I doubt that my mother thought my dress was particularly suitable, either, but there was nothing she could do about it. It was copied from Poiret—white satin with a fringed skirt to give it *un peu de mouvement* and a pearl-and-diamond stomacher to hold the fringe back before it sprang. It looked like the South Sea Islands—like a hula skirt.

How I miss fringe! Where is fringe today? The fringe was there in the twenties—as it was there in the sixties—because of the dancing, the *dancing* . . . the *music!* I've known two great decades in my life, the twenties and the sixties, and I'm always comparing them because of the music. Music is everything, and in those two decades you got something so sharp, so new. . . .

The *tango!* The tango's basically the waltz—you're making a square on the floor all the time—but it's much more stylized. It's a certain way of holding your body, holding your head . . . don't forget the strength it takes to step out. You had to have a marvelous partner. It's a fascinating, totally South American dance. One day, when South America comes through, we'll realize the curious effect it's had on our culture.

A snob might say, "The tango, for God's sake—is that culture?"

By the time I was seventeen, I knew what a snob was. I also knew that young snobs didn't *quite* get my number. I was much better with Mexican and Argentine gigolos (they weren't *really* gigolos —they were just odd ducks around town who liked to dance as much as I did). They were people who knew that I loved clothes, a certain nightlife, and that I *loved* to do the tango.

This naturally was rather un-understood in New York.

I was considered a bit fast. The story got out. The Colony Club's right across the street from here. One afternoon a few years ago I was walking with Andy Warhol. I said, "Look over there, Andy. That's a very select woman's club."

Andy said, "Woman's club? What do they do?"

I said, "Well, I'm not sure. My mother and my grandmother wanted me to join, but I was blackballed, which means you don't get in."

"Why?"

"Well, I was considered fast."

"*Fast!* Gee. They won't let you in if you're *fast?* What do they do in there?" It was the first time I had ever really heard Andy excited.

I said, "They have their hair done, they dictate letters, they have lunch with each other. It's lovely . . . but I'm not a member."

It never mattered to me. At the time my mother was upset. My grandmother had been one of the original founders. But I was much more interested in going to the nightclubs way downtown—to avoid running into my mother and father—and doing what I loved to do best . . . dancing.

In those days my mother was rather un-understood too. Her flamboyance was rather resented. Whispers would go around: "Look, she's painted." She was *very* made up for those days. But men were infatuated with her. There were many scandals, because she was often involved with somebody. She traveled with a very good-looking Turk named Sadi-Bey who wore a red fez with his suit or his dinner jacket. He was absolutely charming. We usually saw him only at night, and he'd arrive in his dinner jacket with the tassel hanging from the fez down over it. We thought he was the height of chic. Though we weren't exactly what you'd call a tidy little group, my parents were devoted to each other. Theirs was a very old-fashioned marriage. A little sort of episode like Sadi-Bey and others—that was nothing.

I remember this: my mother wouldn't have a chauffeur or a footman unless he was infatuated with her—he had to show enormous *dazzle* for her. Everyone had to or she wasn't interested. I can remember at one time saying something extraordinary to her like: "You expect every coachman on the block to be in love with you! What's the matter with you? Don't you ever cool down?"

But she had to be on stage, often making a show of herself. She'd even flirt with *my* boyfriends, and occasionally one would fall flat for her. She was quite young and beautiful and amusing and *mondaine* and splashy, all of which I'm glad I had in my background—*now*. But I've had to live a long time to come to that conclusion.

In my memory, she seems vivid and affectionate and lonely. I think she was someone who was possessed by a great fear. She was even afraid of servants—she was afraid of anything that would disturb anything. Yet she lived only for excitement. When she died, at fifty-two, I think it was because she could find nothing to interest her.

My father was rather amused by her flirtations—it was all part of the scene. Flirtations are part of life, part of society—if one didn't have these little flings, where would one be? I think my father realized this. He was devoted to my mother. She was in the arms of a strong man who saw to everything because he knew that she wasn't strong.

I was much stronger—with a stronger will and a stronger *character*—but I didn't realize it then. All I knew then was that my mother wasn't proud of me. I was always her ugly little monster.

I never felt comfortable about my looks until I married Reed Vreeland.

He was the most beautiful man I've ever seen. He was very quiet, very elegant. I loved all that. I thought it was so beautiful to just watch him.

I met him on the Fourth of July at a weekend party in Saratoga, in 1924. I believe in love at first sight because that's what it was. I knew the moment our eyes met that we would marry.

I simply *assumed* that—and I was right. We became friends, as they say. He was Robert Pruyne's apprentice in the banking business in Albany.

One day, about ten days before the wedding, I was lunching with some friends when the telephone rang and I was called to it.

It was a woman's voice. "Is this Diana Dalziel?" she asked. "I'm a newspaper writer. I've watched you at parties and I've always admired you. You're different from any of the other girls and you have a style all your own. The world is your oyster. This is why I don't want to see you hurt."

I couldn't imagine what all this was leading up to. But the woman went on, "I have to tell you that your mother is being mentioned as a corespondent in a divorce suit and there's going to be an enormous *blaze* in the newspapers."

I heard all this, thanked the woman, and finished my lunch. Naturally, I didn't say a word to the people I was lunching with. But as soon as we'd finished, I telephoned home and found out that my mother had taken the dogs to Central Park. I'd always hated Central Park as a child. It has no secrets, no allure. But I took a cab to the Ramble, where I knew my mother usually went—imagine finding anyone in Central Park today—and when I saw our car and chauffeur, I stopped.

I got out; I walked around behind a hill and found her sitting in the sun with one of our adorable little Scotties in her lap and the other one running around her. She was laughing and talking with them. I sat down beside her and told her exactly what I'd been told.

I felt *nothing*. And that's how she answered me—with *nothing*. She was smaller than me. Very quiet. Then she said, "I think we'll go home. Don't you?"

I don't think I saw her for two or three days. I was very sorry for her.

"All these stories about your mother," my father said to me later, "are untrue. You must simply rise above them." The scandal didn't affect my father nearly as much as it did my mother. Daddy was British in a very healthy way: he could get over things. "Worse things happen at sea." That was his great expression. It summed up any unpleasantness.

That was the end of the story as far as my family went. That's the kind of family we were—very English. Very little visible emotion.

I never saw the newspapers, but the story came out, and obviously it was true. From what I heard later, the man was rather a bigshot in munitions. His name was Sir Charles Ross—Ross Rifles— and he lived in London and Scotland and Africa; the story was filled with guns and excitement and elephants and trips to India and Africa . . . et cetera. It was quite dramatic, and it was in the newspapers every single day.

I was only interested in getting married. The morning of the wedding I went to see my godmother, "Baby Belle" Hunnewell, married to Hollis Hunnewell of Boston. I went to see her because she couldn't come to the church to see me. It was the thing to do. She was in bed. Divine. She supposedly had one less layer of skin than everyone else. Most extraordinary color. *Tiny* bit of pink under the white. Of course, no one was sunburned in those days. She was too beautiful for words. She used to lie in bed and drink gin. She wasn't at all well. She didn't care—she was having a marvelous time. She took two rooms here in New York—fed up with Boston. The big salon she made into a bedroom; at the foot of her bed she tied this great bouquet of balloons. She had the most beautiful nightgowns. They were white handkerchief linen with black lace and then pink satin ribbon threaded through. She was lying in bed with one of her beautiful nightgowns, and for the first time I saw something embroidered right over her left bazoom: a little black bell. And I said, "Oh, Baby Belle, I've never seen that."

"Oh, everything I own has my baby bell on it."

So that was the day of the wedding. I had on the *most* beautiful dress, which I'm sure I still have somewhere—I should give it to the Museum. The bride of this period was the most vulgar bouffant creature, but *my* dress had a very strict line and a very high neckline—very *moyen âge*. There was lace strapped around my head and face, and the train was all *diamanté* and encrusted with pearls. . . .

When I arrived at St. Thomas's Church, my father met me and said, "Not too many people have come, so you will find the church rather . . . sparse."

It wasn't sparse—it was practically empty. Not one invitation to the wedding had been delivered, I was told. They had all been thrown out by mistake. Or perhaps it was because of the scandal that the newspapers had so conveniently not announced it.

To this day, because of this, I don't believe in the free press. The only newspaper I've ever really approved of was *The Times* of London when they had canaries for sale on the front page.

But this made as much difference to me then as it does to you right now. I just wanted to marry Reed Vreeland. Nothing could have spoiled my happiness. I was so proud. You see, I was very young—in every way—and I was marrying an *older* man. He was twenty-five years old, but to me he was an older man, and marrying him was an achievement.

He had fantastic glamour for me. And he always retained it. Isn't it curious that even after more than forty years of marriage, I was always *slightly* shy of him? I can remember his coming home in the evening—the way the door would close and the sound of his step. . . . If I was in my bath or in my bedroom making up, I can remember always pulling myself up, thinking, "I must be at my very best." There was never a time when I didn't have that reaction—*ever*.

The beauty of him was that he looked the same when he died as he had when I married him. His whole stance, his whole allure, his *chemistry* . . . was that of a young man. He was never withered. He never struck age—*ever*.

This is why I can't stand old people. It never occurs to me to be attracted to anyone older, because I've never loved anyone older—except my older man.

Of course, you learn everything from older people. After we were married, Reed and I moved to Albany, where he was training as a banker, and there everyone was older than us. The queen of the town was Lulu Van Rensselaer, who was married to Louis Van Rensselaer, one of the great fascinators of all time. Reed and I were like the little children down the garden path, and we'd be asked to dinner in their great house on the hill on State Street, designed by Stanford White.

One night we went to a dinner at Lulu Van Rensselaer's at which there were two very famous Harvard professors. At the table the talk swung around to Shakespeare. Finally, one of the professors asked, "May I inquire, Mrs. Van Rensselaer, why you insist on pronouncing Cleopatra 'Cle*o*ptra'? It should be 'Cleo*pa*tra,' of course." Mrs. Van Rensselaer drew herself up and announced, "I refer to her as Cle*o*ptra because that is correct." That would seem to have been the end of any argument, but she went on to say, "However, since you are obviously not convinced, I shall write to my old friend President Lowell of Harvard, and he will, of course, give the final word. Two weeks from today—which will give me time to write to the president, and him time to respond—we will all dine here again, exactly the same people at this table. And I will then read you Dr. Lowell's response."

So we all dined two weeks thence. Lulu was in full form, full regalia, sailing like the Armada into the room to receive us. When we got to the dining table, she reached down and took out of her bosom—which could have held *anything*, it was so huge—the letter from the president of Harvard, which she proceeded to read to us.

" 'My dearest Louisa, you are quite correct in believing that Cleopatra's proper pronunciation is "Cle*o*ptra." How interesting to hear from you. I send you my very best regards, blah, blah, blah . . . ' " —and with that she folded the letter and put it back into the vast cleavage of her bosom. Naturally, we never saw the letter, and certainly no one was going in there to look for it. She could have made the whole thing up. She was quite intimidating, and certainly no protest was forthcoming from the Harvard professors, who were shy and rather sheepish—and if Cleopatra had come up again in the conversation, it wouldn't have surprised me at all if *both* of them had begun referring to her as Cle*o*ptra!

Our house was in a little mews that belonged to Mrs. Van Rensselaer back of her State Street mansion. Every door in the mews was painted a different color. Ours was red, and we had blue hydrangeas in sweet little window boxes in front. In those days Albany was a pretty Dutch town—great style! As clean as a Dutch kitchen, and not the vulgar political city it's become. I loved it—this environment of good food, good housekeeping, polished floors, polished brass, servants. . . . My first son, Timmy, was born there, and I was very, very domestic.

Don't think I was always the person you see now. Don't think I was the same person before I started working. I was born lazy. During this phase when I lived in Albany I'd walk around in a mackintosh and a *béret basque* with *very* extreme, very exaggerated makeup—I've always had a strong Kabuki streak. I'd be criticized, but Lulu Van Rensselaer adored it. I loved our life there. I was totally happy. I didn't care what any other place was like. I'd still be there now if Reed hadn't wanted to move to London. I only moved where he wanted to go.

I had nothing to do—but *nothing*.

I never had an idea.

I was like a Japanese wife. When I got to Japan, I realized that someday there's going to be a terrific female revolution there, because for the moment all the women do is housekeep. But a Japanese house, like my little mews house in Albany, can be cleaned in five minutes, so there's very little housekeeping to be done. Of course, there's the arrangement of flowers and so on, but the wife has nothing to do after her husband leaves the house in the morning. He works all day, and then he goes to a geisha house, which is rather like going to a club. He talks business with his cronies while the girls fan him. They have no eyes, they have no ears, they know nothing, see nothing . . . that's a geisha. It isn't sex, you know—it's an entirely different thing. But when the men get home, their days are complete, and the wives have had nothing to do—but *nothing*.

In Kyoto, I was the guest of the chamber of commerce, so I dined with the men every night. It was always in an inn, and we were always seated on the straw matting of the floor, which happens to be very easy for me. The geishas come in and bow to all the men; then they move like butterflies around the room and take their positions on their knees. There's nothing quick about the way they move —it's all very *quiet*. They laugh and they talk and you don't feel out of it not knowing what they're saying because, whatever it is, it's all full of charm—their voices, their faces.

Then . . . as soon as dinner was over, they'd leave the men and circle around me. I'd ask them about their makeup—this is all through an interpreter, of course—because I was so *interested* in how their skin looked after they took off all this heavy stuff which had been on their faces all day. I asked what makeup they used, where they got it—most of it turned out to be Revlon, to tell you the truth. But the point is that they were so charming and so amusing—to *me*, not just to the men.

"Why are these girls so charming to me?" I asked one of the men.

"Because," he said, "the first rule that a geisha is taught, at the age of nine, is to be charming to other women."

I thought this was something we could learn in the West. Every girl in the world should have geisha training.

I know what I'm talking about. I *know*. My God, when I moved to London after Albany, I made great friends among the English during the time I lived there. Those Englishwomen look after Englishmen like nobody's *baby* has ever been looked after, but on the other hand they'll go after anyone's husband themselves. Brother, what I saw *left* and *right*! I certainly had a more attractive husband than most women have. He wasn't that flirtatious, but *they* were, and naturally it was flattering to me . . . up to a *point*.

The point is that Englishwomen are ruthless, whereas geishas aren't ruthless at all. They're totally safe within themselves— which is rather unusual, *mmm*?

But those Japanese wives . . . You've read back through the centuries in *The Tale of Genji* and in *The Pillow Book*—you'll remember that the women lived in beautiful compounds with lattice-work porches like those in Heian paintings where the women's hair is threaded through the bamboo lattice and comes out in another part of the country. But they were pretty idle. They had servants to look after their clothes and their wigs and their makeup, to grind the white powder that they put on their faces—the whole bit. Everything was done for them.

You can't compare the Japanese with anyone else. They're always being compared with the Chinese, who, as you know, were the greatest philosophers, astronomers, astrologers, chemists, the greatest —they go *all the way*! They invented ice cream, fireworks, spaghetti, macaroni, noodles, pug dogs, Pekinese, chows—everything. But all those things are something we totally understand. Something Japanese like hara-kiri, on the other hand, we find impossible to understand. Yet it's as normal to the Japanese as smoking a cigarette.

The whole Japanese thing is so *total*! Think of the sumo wrestlers. While I was there a party was held for me in a large Westernized house outside Kyoto. The high point of the evening was the opening of a huge red brocaded box as tall as you are. I couldn't *imagine* what was inside. I was led forward and asked to open up the paneled door. Oh, brother! Out stepped two sumo wrestlers! They were in full regalia, which is very little, especially in the back. The two were totally glorious. But if looks could kill! They didn't enjoy being on exhibition. I was *so* on their side. I felt very sorry for the boys . . . I mean, how could they stand *being* exhibited in such a way? They're very proud, those sumo wrestlers, extraordinary heritage and history, national *treasures*, and here they were cooped up in a large box, the two of them waiting *God* knows how long in the darkness, waiting for me to open the box so they could step out—big surprise! Well, it *was* a surprise. After all, I'm a Westerner, and a heathen in their eyes, and it was all done for my pleasure to be able to discover these two sumos in a box, like a pair of shoes. They were far from a pair of shoes let me *tell* you. I pretended it was an everyday affair. I put on the biggest smile—as if isn't it interesting to meet someone *new*? I stepped forward and shook hands with each of them. I certainly didn't treat them as if they were stuffed. I mean they may have been miffed, but they were alive. I wanted to hear all about their diets, because they have *such* skin—apricot porcelain, and from the age of nine they eat the same meal, bowl after bowl of the purest ingredients of health. Three times a day.

And then think of the Kabuki Theatre—the extremeness of *that* tradition, so utterly different. Actually, it's only the *instincts* of acting, only the smallest nuances. But it must have great power, because it's been the same since the eighth century.

When I was in Japan, I saw the new star of the Kabuki theatre—a boy who must have been only twenty years old—do a dance in shadow and light that was absolutely extraordinary. I know the routine because I've always been crazy about Kabuki. But when I saw this boy, Tomasaburo Bando, it was as if I'd never seen it before—the coming forward, the going back, the coming forward, the going back, the coming forward, the going back, bringing people forward, pushing people back, bringing people forward, pushing people back . . . and *then*, suddenly, with a twist of the wrist, he flicked open a fan. I was stunned with delight.

He made it look easy, but it isn't easy at all. It takes terrific muscular control—an extraordinary combination of tension and re-laxation—and terrific strength.

This is a *woman* he's playing, you understand—as you know, all the actors are men. But the *delicacy* of this boy . . . it was all in the eyelid, which was more delicate than the first flower of spring. I promise you, if I had a daughter I would send her to him to learn how to become a woman.

CHAPTER
FIVE

We left Albany for London just before the Crash in 1929. We moved into the lovely house in Hanover Terrace. If you live just outside of Europe, as we did, you always find yourself on the move—the glories of the Continent are right at hand.

Have you ever taken one of my little audio guides at the Museum? None of my friends have. My friends never see my shows. "Oh, Diana, it's simply wonderful . . . marvelous." End of conversation. To me, the audio guides are important, because what's the point of going through the show unless you learn something? So you pay your money and you hear me talk. They're really not bad. But the other day I put one on and started listening to myself and I kept going on about Tunisia. *Tunisia*—it was so absurd! Why was I saying this? Why couldn't I shut up? I suppose it's because when Reed and I went to live in Europe we often seemed to be going into a French colony.

We rarely went to the south of France. We never went to the chic *villes d'eau*. You could sit down with other people my age and they could tell you about Deauville, they could tell you about Monte Carlo, they could tell you about . . . dining with the King of Spain! We never did any of these things. We'd go to North Africa.

Or we'd go to Bavaria or to Hungary. We only went where the air was fragrant and life was easy. We traveled rather luxuriously in our glorious Bugatti with our marvelous chauffeur and my maid from London, and there was never any problem.

Of course, there were things we missed. We never went to Spain when Alfonso XIII was King. God knows, we were asked. Years later, Spanish friends used to say to me, "Diana, you always miss the boat. You should have been here when Alfonso was King. Then you would have seen *Spain*."

Alfonso—that gorgeous, glorious, marvelous Bourbon! I met him—once—in London, before he went into exile. He was the most exciting man I'd ever seen. There was no one like the King of Spain. You know that he was the only man ever *born* King of Spain—he was born *after* his father's death. The King of Spain was . . . well, the King of Spain . . . this shiny, magnificent man. He had the Spanish Bourbon nose, and that mouth which was set *up* and *out*. His mustache was marvelous, his hair was rich and black, he was a bit dark, he loved dogs, horses, men, women. . . . You'd never think anything in the world could go wrong for him. But then think of what his last years were like. Do you realize that nobody would walk on the same side of the street with him in Rome? It was supposed to be bad luck. The evil eye.

Alfonso married Victoria Eugenia—"Ena" of Battenberg, this marvelous, totally chic granddaughter of Queen Victoria and god-daughter of the Empress Eugénie. She introduced hemophilia into the family, and each of their sons—except one—was born with some terrible physical defect. They were deaf, they were dumb, they had club feet—they had everything.

And Alfonso had to go when the monarchy went and the Civil War began. He was thrown out of the country like an old boot. He left by battleship the way Edward VIII left England when he abdicated.

One day Reed and I were motoring through the south of France to Marseilles. We arrived at the Hôtel de Noailles, where we were going to spend the night. The next morning we were going to take a boat to Sidi Bou Saïd in Tunisia. That night, we'd arranged to go on a tour of the red-light district of Marseilles with the prefect of police. It was a very interesting evening we were going to have.

After we settled ourselves in our room, Reed went downstairs to see about our evening's prowl, and I sort of dozed off. I felt that the hotel was abuzz with something, but I was really too sleepy to think about anything. Reed rang up from downstairs. "Please," he said, "don't, under any circumstances, come down until I've come up."

As we were going downstairs together, he said, "Here's what I have to tell you: the King of Spain arrived this morning by battleship, and he's here with—"

No sooner had he said it than I *saw* it. The entire court of Spain had arrived. The whole palace had been kicked out of Spain, and here they were in the Hôtel de Noailles. In the ballroom we saw the little Infantes and Infantas on stretchers . . . in braces, in wheelchairs, most of them in some way disabled. There were older children; old servant women carrying baskets, wandering aimlessly through the lobby . . . there was everybody there who is in any royal family. It was like cleaning out an attic. They all had rooms; everything had been arranged. They weren't like refugees, yet they lived the rest of their lives as refugees.

So we left the royal family, moving through that extraordinary scene, and off we went on our evening's prowl . . . into a world so utterly different.

We were now five—Reed and I, Kitty and Perry Brownlow, who were going to Tunisia with us, and the prefect of police.

"I do want you to know," the prefect said, "that the British consul disappeared five weeks ago while doing rather the same thing that you're about to do, prowling through the red-light district of our city—and he hasn't been heard from since. Are you still prepared to go?"

Listen, can a duck swim? What the hell did we care?

"Yes," I said.

So we made our first stop. We went through this very dark alley, and against the walls were these Pepe le Mokos. The only thing you'd see was the ends of their cigarettes—their bodies were against the wall in shadows. From the alley we passed into these inner, secret squares within squares of *such* a magnificence, *such* a scale, *such* a proportion—they must have been early Renaissance—but all in darkness.

Then, in the innermost square, we saw, floodlit, a palace façade with stone pediments and balustrades carved with pyramids and the most beautiful, enormous door you ever saw. Do we go in that door? Forget it—this is a tale of *vice!* We went in the lowliest little doorway at the side, where we were met by the madam, who was quite padded out and had a mustache about the size of Adolphe Menjou's.

"*Bonsoir, bonsoir!*" she said in this terrific accent, the Marseillaise, which is very hard to understand, even with something as simple as "*bonsoir.*" She went on: "You're here to see the movies, you're here to see the action, you're here to see the girls—what?"

"Everything!" the prefect said.

This brothel was called the Edward VII. Every good brothel in Europe was called the Edward VII. He liked them very much and sort of christened them as he went along. Apparently, this was his favorite, or so we were told—how do I know if there's any truth to it? I'm only telling you what we *saw.* We saw silver rooms, we saw gold rooms, we saw rooms of mirrors . . . and then we went into an enormous red-and-gold Edward VII ballroom with little gold chairs all around and a band tuning up, led by this little hunchback.

Then the girls came in and took their seats. It didn't look like much of an evening for them—three guys and two girls had arrived, so where were they to fit in? But the prefect was marvelous, talking to this obscene woman with the Adolphe Menjou mustache—this buxom, army-captain sort of a woman.

Then . . . the band strikes up. The bandleader, we were told—this little hunchback at the piano—was the leader of the orchestra of the Marseilles Opera. He was the most important musician in Marseilles, and every night he played for the girls.

It was *too* extraordinary. Shall we say *that's* what's attractive about brothels? They're where earth and sky meet.

"Oh, my *God*," I said to Reed when we finally got back to the hotel, "what an evening! The gnome, the girls, the madam, the old servant women carrying baskets, the little Infantes, the little Infantas . . . the *King of Spain!*"

We never did find out what happened to the British consul.

This was all *one day*. It may sound like too much of an experience, but don't forget, we were living every hour of that day. Everything was a lot in those days. The world was much larger—and much smaller. Don't ask me to explain that.

But don't think you were born too late. Everyone has that illusion. But you aren't. The only problem is if you *think* too late.

That was my mother's problem, and that was her tragedy. She used to write Reed and me letters on our honeymoon in Paris: "My dear darling children, I cry for you in the rain when I think that you missed all the glories of Paris before the war, when I think that you never saw the Bois as it was, when I think. . . ."

"Glory be to *God!*" I said. I wrote her back the most terrible letter: "Dear Mother, Were you ever in the Galerie des Glaces? Did you ever know what it was to be presented to Louis XIV? Did you ever hunt the stag with the bugles and the hounds of Henri II in the forest of Fontainebleau? Forget it! Anything I'm missing today I'd like to know the name of!"

Naturally, she never in her life referred to my letter.

Everything is new. At least everything is new the first time around.

So Reed and I made a point of going to out-of-the-way new places. To some, naturally, we were invited. Baron Rodolphe d'Erlanger was the one who invited us to Sidi Bou Saïd after our adventure in Marseilles. He couldn't be called the black sheep of the d'Erlanger family—he was a perfectly enchanting man—but he was an odd bird. He never went into the d'Erlanger bank, which was as queer as if you decided to walk on your hands rather than on your legs. His wife,

Bettina, was a Roman beauty with turquoise eyes. The two had gone to Sidi Bou Saïd as bride and groom, and they adored their life there so much they stayed and built a very beautiful house—a miniature palace. Their friends, who were the most interesting people in Europe, came to visit them—Elsie Mendl, for instance, was there during that first visit Reed and I made. We'd never been to Africa before, and I was so *excited*. It was dawn when we arrived in Sidi Bou Saïd. From the deck I saw the d'Erlangers' house—a little white palace, actually, on the top of a white cliff rising straight out of the Mediterranean, terraced all the way up from the sea with gardens of orange trees, lemon trees, and oleanders.

We docked. Then we made our way to the palace, and in the courtyard we saw menservants. We only saw menservants the whole time we were there, *dressed* . . . and in the evening they'd *redress*, and it was like the Arabian Nights—these great big pantaloons with gold and silver brocade and lamé boleros worn over very clean white shirts.

We walked past the menservants into a hall with orange marble walls and a mauve marble ceiling supported by sixteenth-century lace columns, made of a stone that's carved like lace and *is called* lace. Between the columns were little birds flying in and out, in and out . . . and there was a tiny rivulet running through the hall with gardenias floating in it.

Then we went into lunch—European, in that you sat at a pink marble table set with gold goblets. I sat on the right of Baron Rodolphe, who always had a beautiful linen handkerchief—like an absolutely transparent cobweb—which never left his hand and which he'd raise to his nose . . . he was an ether addict.

"Diana . . . [*sniff*]," he'd say, "it's so wonderful to see you looking so *well*. You're the night's morning . . . [*sniff*], you're the sun, the moon, and the *stars* . . . [*sniff, sniff*]"—you know, the sort of business that men say to women by the sea.

"Reed," I once said, "what happens if I really get a *blast* of it?"

"You won't," he said. "Just remember—when he breathes *in*, you breathe *out*."

Rodolphe was so *attractive*. Don't think this ritual of his was *unattractive*—it just took a little getting used to. This little weakness for ether was as normal as if you . . . Listen, Baron Rodolphe was the uncrowned King of Tunisia!

His best friend was Fuad, the King of Egypt, King Farouk's father. Together, they were really responsible for getting the music of the Arabs of North Africa onto paper. They'd work on the music together in Baron Rodolphe's beautiful library, and they'd exchange orchestras. Sometimes, when we came in to dinner, the orchestra would be playing, and it would play through dinner and into the night. . . .

Every morning, everyone would go down to the sea for a swim, through the gardens, past a herd of peacocks. Everyone else went together, and I guess the peacocks felt they could let them have their way. But they didn't with me. I was always the last in the morning—I'm *always* the last—so I went down alone, through an acre of lemon and orange orchards, and there'd always be a peacock standing in the way with his tail spread out. "Please let me go by," I'd say. "They're all waiting for me. I won't have time for a swim before lunch. *Please*."

He'd wait until he got good and ready, then he'd put down his tail and *drag* himself back into the orchard.

Peacocks, I always say, are unbelievably beautiful—but they're vulgar. All of these peacocks, however, were silvery white, and I'll tell you why. Apparently, years before, King Fuad—like someone in the sixteenth century—had had sent by special messenger a little woven gold basket containing a pair of little blue peacocks. Naturally, they had babies. Then the babies came and the babies came, and one day there was a white peacock. Then there was another one. And as the herd grew larger and larger, there were more and more white peacocks.

By the time we arrived there must have been seventy-five. The d'Erlangers had given away all the blue peacocks, and as white peacocks only breed other white peacocks, they were white, white, *white*. In the evening they were so beautiful. The top of the palace was flat, and on hot nights we'd go up there after dinner to get the air and look down at the peacocks with their tails spread and their *tiny* heads against the reflection of the moon shining on the sea . . . it didn't look real. When *I* say it didn't look real, it *didn't* look real. It looked like an Aubrey Beardsley drawing for *Salome*.

One night we heard drums. They were to announce that Denys Finch Hatton had died. He was one of the original Great White Hunters. He was a great friend of my mother and of everyone of her generation, and, most important, he was the lover of Isak Dinesen. She was a great friend of mine. Whenever she came to America, she'd come to see me. Every Saturday afternoon she came for tea. Tea was always combined with an early dinner, and she always wanted the same menu. A bottle of champagne. A bunch of grapes. And twelve oysters on the half-shell. She was tortured with illness and operations, but she always got where she wanted to go. She had been dying for twenty years of syphilis.

One snowy Saturday afternoon, the bell rang. I went to answer the door, and there she was standing like a woodsman with a big bunch of bright scarlet gladiolas slung on her shoulder—in the middle of winter, with snow up to your hip. Roaring with laughter, she said, "I brought you some red flowers for a red room," and she threw them at me as if to say, "Good God, I'm glad to get rid of these!"

CHAPTER SIX

I was always fascinated by the absurdities and the luxuries and the snobbism of the world that the fashion magazines showed. Of course, it's not for everyone. Very few people had ever breathed the pantry air of a house of a woman who wore the kind of dress *Vogue* used to show when I was young. But I lived in that world, not only during my years in the magazine business but for years before, because I was always *of* that world—at least in my imagination.

Condé Nast was a very extraordinary man, of *such* a standard. He had a vision. He decided to raise the commercial standards of the American woman. Why, he decided, shouldn't they have the best-looking clothes? He gave them *Vogue*. The best-looking houses? *House & Garden*. And don't forget *Vanity Fair!* Why, Condé decided, shouldn't American women know about writers, entertainers, painters —that Picasso was painting extraordinary paintings, that a man named Proust was writing an extraordinary book? Why shouldn't they know . . . about *Josephine Baker?*

I knew about Josephine Baker. I'd seen her in Harlem. I was never out of Harlem in the early twenties. The *music* was so great, and Josephine was simply the only girl you saw in the chorus line. Her *eyes* were the softest brown velvet, loving, caressing, embracing—all you could feel was something good coming from her. But her eyes were full of laughter, too. She had that . . . *thing*—that's all.

One night I was invited to a Condé Nast party. Everybody who was invited to a Condé Nast party stood for something. He was the man who created the kind of social world that was then called Café Society: a carefully chosen mélange—no such thing as an overcrowded room, mind you—mingling people who up to that time would never have been seen at the same social gathering. Condé picked his guests for their talent, whatever it was—literature, the theatre, *big* business. Sharp, chic society. Why was I asked? I was young, well dressed, and could dance.

This was the Night of the Three Bakers. First, there walked into Condé's party Mrs. George Baker, the wife of the great banker, who was the best-dressed, most attractive woman in New York and a great hostess. *Then* . . . we had *Edythe* Baker, who was the cutest thing in town. She came from Missouri, was rather small, and had an absolutely sublime gift for the piano. In the Cochran Revue in London she had played a huge piano which seemed literally the length of the entire stage. At the keyboard was this little doll, her fingers running up and down as she played and sang "The Birth of the Blues." That was Edythe.

Then, into our midst walked . . . *Josephine* Baker. Now *that* was historic: we have a *black* in the house. Her hair had been done by Antoine, the famous hairdresser of Paris, like a Greek boy's—these small, flat curls against her skull—and she was wearing a white Vionnet dress, cut on the bias with four points, like a handkerchief. It had no opening, no closing—you just put it over your head and it came to you and moved with the ease and the fluidity of the body. And did Josephine *move*! These *long* black legs, these *long* black arms, this *long* black throat . . . and pressed into her flat black curls were white silk butterflies. She had the chic of Gay Paree.

I was so thrilled to be asked. There was no living with me for days. The Night of the Three Bakers!

One night in Paris, after I was married, a friend and I went to a little theatre above Montmartre to see a German movie called

L'Atlantide, with a wonderful actress in it called Brigitte Helm, who played the Queen of the Lost Continent. It was the middle of July. It was *hot.* The only seats in the theatre were in the third balcony, under the rafters, where it was even *hotter.* There were four seats in a row, and we took two.

We sat there, the movie started . . . and I became *totally* intoxicated by it. I was mesmerized! I have no idea if I actually saw the movie I thought I was seeing, but I was absorbed by these three lost Foreign Legion soldiers with their camels, their woes . . . they're so *tired,* they're delirious with dehydration. . . . And then you see the fata morgana. That means if you desire a woman, you see a woman, if you desire water, you see water—everything you dream, you see. But you never reach it. It's all an illusion.

Then . . . a sign of an oasis! There's a palm . . . and more palms. Then they're *in* the oasis, where they see Brigitte Helm, this *divine*-looking woman seated on a throne—*surrounded by cheetahs!* The cheetahs bask in the sun. She fixes her eyes on the soldiers. One of them approaches her. She gives him a glass of champagne and he drinks it. Then she takes the glass from him, breaks it, cuts his *throat* with it. . . .

And et cetera.

This goes on and on. I hadn't moved an inch. At some point I moved my hand . . . to here . . . where it stayed for the rest of the movie. I was spellbound because the mood was so *sustained.* I was simply sucked in, *seduced* by this thing of the desert, *seduced* by the Queen of the Lost Continent, the wickedest woman who ever lived . . . and her cheetahs! The essence of movie-ism.

Then . . . the lights went on, and I felt a slight movement under my hand. I looked down—and it was a *cheetah*! And beside the cheetah was Josephine *Baker!*

"Oh," I said, "you've brought your cheetah to see the cheetahs!"

"Yes," she said, "that's exactly what I did."

She was alone with the cheetah on a lead. She was so beautifully dressed. She was wearing a marvelous little short black skirt and a little Vionnet shirt—no sleeves, no back, no front, just crossed bars on the bias. Dont forget how hot it was, and of course the great thing was to get *out* of this theatre we were in. The cheetah, naturally, took the lead, and Josephine, with those *long* black legs, was *dragged* down three flights of stairs as fast as she could go, and that's *fast*.

Out in the street there was an enormous white-and-silver Rolls-Royce waiting for her. The driver opened the door; she let go of the lead; the cheetah *whooped*, took *one* leap into the back of the Rolls, with Josephine right behind; the door closed . . . and they were off!

Ah! What a gesture! I've never seen anything like it. It was speed at its best, and style. Style was a great thing in those days.

CHAPTER
SEVEN

If I may say so, at least to you, I sometimes think there's something *wrong* with white people. We're in the *wrong* place at the *wrong* time. Blacks are almost the only people I can stand to look at nowadays.

I love to see the black schoolchildren who come into the Museum, marching in a neat little row, wearing immaculate cardigan sweaters their mothers have knitted for them.

The young black girls I see in New York today are the most attractive girls—from top to toe! Their hands are the most beautiful things on *earth*—they always have been. But these girls' *legs* are so extraordinary! They used to stand with their behinds out. You know the walk—they'd sort of sink into their stomachs and then stick out their behinds. But these girls today haven't got a *trace* of it. They stand *tall*, and when they *stride* . . . they're like a race of gazelles! They're strong. They've got the *strength*.

The world will go to lines of color—there's no question about it. It won't be just the Africans and it won't be just the Arabs and it won't be just the Chinese—it will be every part of the world that has any streak of color other than white. The Western world will go. It won't happen in my lifetime, and it may not happen in the next five hundred years, but it will happen. The West is *boring* itself to death! And talking itself to death!

I'm so aware of this change every time I go to Paris and stay at the Crillon. In the sixties when I was covering the collections for *Vogue*, I arrived one evening at the Crillon and the whole of Chad was there. They were *totally* biblical in their tiny caps and their long silver and gold robes to the ground.

Then, the next time, a few years later, I arrived at the Crillon and there was the whole of Africa—but I mean the *whole* of Africa. We had the entourages of about forty countries. They all spoke French and English. The men all wore beautifully cut French suits and French cuffs, and their manners were marvelous.

And the *women* at night! They were too attractive. They all looked like goddesses of the Nile. There's something ancient and marvelous and wonderful about their beautiful gold rings and their beautiful features and their wonderful soft skin. They've got *presence*.

Then . . . the next day, we got the big brass from the Third World—five presidents and one *emperor*! It was fantastico! The robes! The jewels! The security men! The security at the Crillon has always been something fantastic because there are always potentates staying there. I love security men—I just *adore* them. They're hardly there for me, but when I get out of the lift and twenty men stand up, it makes me feel so *safe*.

When the Africans left, there was a quiet around the place that was almost uncanny. *Then* . . . after two days, we got *les arabes*! My *God*, they were the most gorgeous things—all guests of the President of France. You have no idea how beautifully dressed *they* were. And they were so *clean*. It was the cleanest display of white robes I've ever seen. And under the robes they all wore these wonderful little sashes of scarlet and violet. They're young, they're narrow, they're beautifully boned, with wonderful strong noses and beautifully kept beards. And the way they *walk* . . . ! They're *quelqu'uns*, no question.

Then . . . that night, *they* were all wearing djellabas! They had on *brown* ones—hundreds of them! Well, not really djellabas . . . and not really caftans . . . they're sort of an overcoat—these were in thin brown wool piped in gold. . . . I don't know exactly what they are called, but I do know they all had them and *I* want one. I might write a little sort of fan letter to say that all my life I've wanted one in brown. I've got to get a message through.

Ah! What men! They're great gentlemen. They just look straight ahead—they never notice you. Of course, they're rich—*terribly*. And never a woman in sight! Oh, how I'd like to be a concubine kept hidden away in the desert somewhere with *nothing* to think about. . . .

You may notice I'm talking about the blacks and *les arabes* interchangeably now. One day, while the Russian show was on at the Metropolitan Museum, my friend Whitney Warren from San Francisco called and asked if he could bring his friends the Romanovs from San Francisco to see it. So he arrived with his friends—charming, adorable people—and they went *straight* to the blackamoor that we had in the show. They stood in front of this beautiful, *enormous* mannequin, absolutely *mesmerized*. "Madame," they said—speaking French, like all Russian émigrés—"*c'est un arabe!* Oh, how we loved our *arabes!*"

Of course, this blackamoor was about as Arabic as *I* am. . . . But this is a very Russian thing. Remember that blacks played a very important part in the early ballets of Diaghilev, and remember that wonderful book of Pushkin's, *The Emperor's Negro.* Pushkin's grandmother, as you know, was black. Beside every door in all the royal palaces stood a real blackamoor, gigantic, beloved by all the household, there to open and close the doors and keep out the appalling cold.

They have been commemorated in jewelry, in Russia, Venice, very eighteenth and nineteenth century.

Have I ever showed you my little blackamoor heads from Cartier with their enameled turbans? Baba Lucinge and I used to wear them in rows and *rows* . . . they were the *chic* of Paris in the late thirties. When I moved to New York, I made arrangements for the Paris Cartier to sell them to the New York Cartier, and all I can tell you is that the *race* across the ocean—this was by boat, don't forget—was something so *fierce*. The Cartier ones were quite expensive, but then Saks brought out a copy of them that sold for something like, in those days, thirty dollars apiece, and it was impossible to tell them apart. So I bought the copies and wore them with the real ones, like decorations—I was *covered* in blackamoors!

I'm told it's not in good taste to wear blackamoors anymore, but I think I'll revive them. Why not? I think those blacks I see around town today would get a kick out of it . . . *knowing* they're the most beautiful things alive. My escorts say, "What are you looking to do? What are you trying to prove?" But I think the blacks would be jolly amused. They've got sense.

CHAPTER
EIGHT

I wore blackamoors the way Peggy Hopkins Joyce wore diamonds. She was a good-looking blonde—everyone's favorite golddigger in the twenties and thirties. My God, you've never seen such quantities of diamonds as Peggy Hopkins Joyce had! They were great, flat baguettes all the way. My God, she was racy and attractive! Naturally, like everybody who drinks too much champagne, she began to get chins—but she kept her figure pretty well. She genuinely liked the boys.

She was famous for getting money out of the men who went out with her. She'd have her car waiting—she wouldn't drive in *your* car. You'd leave the Ritz in her car, go right to her place for supper or something, and then, back at the Ritz, as you got out again, she'd look at you. "Now what are you going to do for George?" George was the chauffeur who was holding the door open. She knew whom she was dealing with; she wasn't taking this from the kids on the street. That's what she'd say. "What are you going to do for George?" Anything less than a hundred-dollar bill, forget it! At least seven or eight men told me that. Think what a hundred dollars was in *those* days!

George must have been somewhat different from the usual chauffeur. He was more like what we refer to these days as a "driver." Today it's a privilege to have a driver. He looks after you. He's a pretty good friend. He calls you by your first name, you call him by his. In those days, you dressed the chauffeur up—furs in winter, splendid caps—and you called him by his last name: Pollard, Perkins. Peggy didn't, but then she had her own ways and means.

What a generation that was! It was the martini era. In those days, people would get out of the car to see you home, and they'd weave around a bit and fall down on the sidewalk. You'd walk into your house, and they were out there on the sidewalk; and inevitably the chauffeur or the taxi driver would come after them. It was so appalling, the martini of the twenties. If I gave you some gin with a drop of vermouth that wouldn't cover the head of a pin, that would be the martini. The people who drank them were carried home, usually unconscious. I'm only talking about the two or three years when I was kind of on the loose before I got married. I've never seen so much drinking in my life. That's why it's never been remotely attractive to me, but I do understand drunks.

Then, of course, Prohibition came along. Insane idea. Try to keep me from taking a swallow of this tea, and I'll drink the whole pot. Roosevelt knew what to do: repeal. It's hard to believe now that Prohibition ever existed—it seems like a fairy tale.

In 1931, right in the middle of all this, I'd come back from England to New York for a few days without Reed. I fell in love with a place called the Abbaye, which was what used to be known as a "bottle club." That meant you'd be admitted by someone looking at you through an eyehole in the door; you'd go down a long, very dark flight of stairs, bringing your own bottle, which would then be served to you in bouillon cups. People in those days drank bouillon by the *quart*.

It was after the Crash, but it was still a very opulent time in New York. None of the friends I went to the Abbaye with that night seemed to be affected by the Crash, and when I tell you who they were you'll understand why: Tommy Hitchcock—the greatest polo player of all time—and his charming wife, Peggy; Averell Harriman; Sonny Whitney and his divine wife, Marie—the polo group—and a few extra men. So we arrived . . . the richest, swellest group—I'm talking about money-in-the-*bank* rich, not stockbrokers—and everyone was beautifully dressed for dinner. I was *nuts* about the Abbaye—the size of the room, which was very small, the music . . . and, of course, there was a certain element of *danger* because we were in a speakeasy, doing something that was against the law—which didn't *really* interest me, but you can't deny its appeal. It was chic and amusing, and I thought it was all very, very attractive. In there, in this one small room, were the best of all worlds and the worst—a delicious balance if you really like nightlife, as I always have.

So in the Abbaye we were drinking bouillon, bouillon, bouillon—there was no *end* to the bouillon. One of the extra men, a charming Irishman called Jim—I can't remember his last name—decided to get *good* and loaded. Don't think this wasn't attractive. He's since disappeared off the face of the earth, but he was always loaded and always *divine*. So that night he looked across the room and said, "Do you see what I see?"

What he saw was a girl with straight red hair to her shoulders, bangs in front, sloe eyes, a beautiful red dress. He crossed the room to ask her to dance. He was completely *gone*, but he could stand and walk and all that, so he kept talking to her because that's how you handled a pickup in those days. You kept at it even when she'd say, "Oh, that's so sweet of you, but, you see, I've just developed this terrible migraine. . . ."

"Really, Jim," I said, when he came back to the table to get himself resupplied, "you've got to contain yourself. Have you any idea who's sitting there with her?"

"What the hell do I care who's sitting with her?" he said. "That's the girl for *me*."

So he went over to the table for the *second* time, and the man beside the girl stood up, and his *goons* stood up—and there were guns, guns, *guns*. It was Legs Diamond, and the girl was his famous moll, Kiki Roberts. Legs opened his coat. There on his chest were two guns in their holsters. He patted them. Beautiful timing. The elegance of the gesture! His friends all looked up. Baby Face Nelson, Pretty Boy Floyd . . . I can't remember who they all were. But I did know *that* night. So did my friend. He came back very quietly and sat back down at the table and had himself another bouillon or so.

The next night we all went back to the Abbaye—this same little precious crowd of ours—and all the gangsters and the Mafia of the town were in there too, except this time no one from our table bothered them. We knew better. We were sitting there, *roaring* with laughter, having the time of our lives . . . it may have been half past two, it may have been half past three—at that time I'd stay out all night and never know *what* time it was—when suddenly all the lights went out. They came back on again . . . then out—*black*. Then on again . . . then *black*. Now we all knew that three blackouts meant—the cops! So all the flasks disappeared, the bouillon was gulped down, everything was suddenly terribly *comme il faut*—we were all there having a little dinner. There were three cops standing in the middle of the room. "Ladies and gentlemen," one of the cops said, "there will be no checks issued—just go quietly. And when I say 'quietly' "—all three cops had machine guns pulled—"I mean *quietly.*"

So we walked out . . . through the little dark hall, through the door to the sidewalk, out the front, over three men lying there on the stairs, bleeding to death. Apparently, they'd been shot by guns with silencers—we hadn't heard it. But there was no other way to walk out, carefully stepping over them to the street.

I can remember *exactly* what I had on that night—a white satin dress and white satin slippers. Of course, one always dressed in those days. You dressed if you went to Harlem, you dressed if you went to a bottle club. Well, to walk home with blood-spattered white satin slippers . . . I've never forgotten it—the Night of the Abbaye.

Of course, Prohibition was a time when there tended to be a *lot* of excitement. It was because you weren't allowed to drink that you drank anything you could get your hands on. People would go into the bathroom and drink Listerine! Anything that might have a crrrumb of alcohol. They were such attractive men. So many, many died of drink. They didn't last very long.

Reed and I spent most of Prohibition in London, but in the summer of 1928 we stayed at my father-in-law's house in Brewster,

New York. I was out on the lawn with my little tiny bambino Frecky. It was simply divine! Well, you know how you feel about your children. He was lying in the sun and he was the color of mahogany and very chatty. Always good humor, always adorable. And huge! He was eleven pounds and a half, just imagine, when he was born. I am sort of a case, you know. It was apparently in all the medical research because of my slight size. I had two children: Timmy was born in fourteen minutes, and Frecky was born in seven minutes. No before pains or anything, just born. Over! It's very handy. Apparently, my size didn't affect me one way or the other; I simply knew it was the only way.

Anyway, I was sitting there in the sun talking to my darling bambino, and this marvelous-looking man drew up in a car, got out, went straight to the house—I was out on the lawn—and took quite a big package and left it inside. Then he walked out and came by. He said, "Mrs. Vreeland?" And I said, "Yes?"

He wore the most beautiful clothes, marvelous tailoring, beautiful hat; those were the days when men wore fedoras. Brewster was very rustic in those days: we were on three dirt roads and all that. He said, "I'm ——" whoever it is—Joe Palooka. "I'm your husband's bootlegger. Reed and I are great friends. I'm pleased to meet you. What a beautiful child you have"—blah, blah, blah. I was thinking: God, what beautiful clothes. Gee, these wops, they know how to put their tailors to work. He was very charming. I said, "Oh, sit down with me. You don't have to rush back to New York."

So we sat there, and talked, and *guess what happened!* There was a faint droning noise overhead, and we looked up and Charles Lindbergh flies over us! En route to Paris! Charles Lindbergh. I always said to Frecky that it was a very lucky sort of sign. We had looked up and seen this plane. Of course, the sky wasn't filled with planes in those days. I said to Frecky, "Really, what a wonderful sort of hour: to be in the sunshine, to be totally happy, giggling and bubbling and carrying on like babies do, and I'm sitting there with your father's bootlegger, and *Lindbergh* flies over!"

CHAPTER
NINE

You should really be talking to Joseph, my masseur. There's someone who knows the inside stuff. There's someone who's had a *life*. He was the masseur of Mistinguett, of Josephine Baker . . . listen, he lived at Buckingham Palace!

When Josephine Baker had a very bad accident doing splits at the Casino de Paris, tearing all the ligaments up to here, Joseph got permission from Queen Mary to cross the Channel three times a week, and he *melded* her ligaments back to where they belong. He's still the same today. He just happens to have healing power in his hands.

"Now, Joseph," I'll say, "what did you do for Queen Mary?"

"Oh, madame," he'll reply—speaking this heavy, *guttural* Alsatian French—"she opened every day sixteen bazaars—something terrible!"

"Oh," I'll say, "well, then you just massaged her feet."

"Oh no, madame! I did *everything*! I had to start . . . here."

"And what did she wear?"

"Oh, madame . . ."

"Now, Joseph, what did she wear?"

"Nothing."

"Now, Joseph, I don't believe you. Queen Mary never, *never* was massaged with nothing on."

"Madame, I tell you—she wore *nothing* when she was massaged by me!"

I had these conversations with Joseph all the time.

But these are things you can't say. You can't say "My masseur told me this." And then again, why can't you?

I *can* tell you what it was to be presented at court—that was *something*. It took hours and hours—before you even got there. So you took food and you took a flask. And you sat forever, because all the cars were held up in the Mall, with all of London looking in at you and saying " 'Ere's to you, dearie!" and "Cheerio, duckie!" and all that divine Cockney stuff.

Then . . . you got there, and it was the most wonderful thing, I suppose, that there could be in the world to see. The ceremony is held in a *huge* square room, the throne room—I've always thought a square room is the most beautiful—and at the far end was a platform. On one side of the platform were the Scots in their tartans, their laces, their velvets, their daggers, their sporrans . . . you know, they're worn to keep the kilts down—otherwise they'd fly in the wind. They *do* fly in the wind, by the way. I can tell you. My sister and I had quite an upbringing in Scotland. When gentlemen bent over to stoke the peat fire . . . there wasn't much *we* didn't know about.

In any case, here were the Scots in all their regalia . . . and *here* were the two royals, King George V and Queen Mary, who were, I suppose, the most royal people in memory—nothing against the present Queen, but there was something about those two that was *total*, because they were Emperor and Empress of India, and the sun never set on English soil. And *there*, on the other side of the platform, were the *Indians* in all *their* regalia, with their sapphires, their pearls —their wealth in pearls was incredible—their emeralds, and their rubies. Brocades, tunics, pantaloons—though perhaps that's too Turkish a descriptive. In any case, it was luxury *in depth*.

Just beside the two thrones was a boy who must have been
seventeen years old. I'd never seen him before. He was exactly the
color of a gardenia. A gardenia isn't *quite* white. It's got a little cream
in it. You can't say a white person has gardenia skin. But he did. And
his eyes were *black*. He was dressed in an eighteenth-century coat
of white brocade with pale blue, pink, green, and yellow flowers—
to the knees—and tight white satin trousers. His head, which was
bound in a turban, was absolutely beautiful and very wide for its
smallness—it was a little face. This was the first time I ever saw
Aly Khan.

But I only bring this up to tell you about a person who was
standing even nearer to Their Majesties on the dais.

One night, a few years before this, Leo d'Erlanger had asked
Reed and me to dine in what in those days was known as a "club."
Not a true men's club like White's or Boodle's. These "clubs" were
practically brothels—not that that's what they were used for, but they
were like brothels in that there was no visible exit or entrance. It was
the kind of place where J. P. Morgan could dine luxuriously in total
privacy. You'd go in a side door, and they were . . . discreet. Leo was
dining with someone he wanted to do business with, and he asked us
to come as a favor.

The man's name was Nubar Gulbenkian. He was the son
of the financier who made a billion dollars or so in oil—Calouste
Gulbenkian—Mr. Five Percent. Now I knew that his father had the
greatest collection of Chinese art in the world and that, having collected the Orient, he was starting in on these fantastic European
pictures the world now knows—like the Rubens of the woman with
the black servant holding an umbrella over her head, and et cetera.
Naturally, I was *spellbound*.

I can't say the son was very impressive, though there was
nothing *wrong* with him. But for some reason he took quite a fancy to
me. And from that time on, when he'd see me across every nightclub
and across every lobby during every entr'acte at the opening of every
play all over London, he made quite a stir about it.

"Ah! Diana!" he'd shout across the room, tearing up a napkin.

"*Really*, Diana," my English friends would say in lowered voices, "the people that you pick up!"

"I didn't pick him up," I'd say. "I was *introduced*."

That was as far as he and I went. In later years he became very chic—he always had a green orchid in his buttonhole—but by this time he was well out of my life. It had been just a few small moments in theatres, in nightclubs . . . all the cheap stuff.

Let's get back to court. I've just made my curtsy to King George and Queen Mary. Now I happen to love curtsying. I was brought up British, don't forget. And also I like to extend my extremities. I was halfway down in the curtsy department, and then, of course, you have to get yourself *up*. If you live in London, you don't just make this little bob—you go *all the way* down and then all the way *up*. I was just coming up when suddenly my eye was *stretched* as I looked at one of the great royal jewels in the world. One would never forget it once one's seen it. It has a very extraordinary cut: it's almost mirror cut, that is to say flat, like a baguette. Of course, the great value in a diamond is its thickness. Well, I'm talking about something that was built like an egg and cut flat with the light, very sharp, just *pouring* out. I stared at it. I didn't think I could finish my curtsy.

Then I took in who was wearing it. He was wearing a huge black turban, a marvelous black djellaba . . . it was my friend Nubar Gulbenkian. I couldn't have been more surprised—this man who had shouted at me and "shamed" me in all those theatre lobbies standing there beside the *throne*. I don't know what startled me more—the man being where he was or the astonishing jewel he wore. Why *he* was wearing it I did not know.

Then, a lord-in-waiting who was a great friend of Adele Astaire Cavendish's—a charming chap, all turned out for court in knee britches—came up to me and said, "Adele told me you were being presented tonight. May I take you into the diplomatic buffet, where the lords- and ladies-in-waiting will be having their supper?"

I was *enchantée*, naturally.

So we went in. There was a light entertainment and these beautiful little sandwiches and the *bouillon* . . . I'll never forget it. And then, by God, this man Gulbenkian, who had *demeaned* me in every theatre lobby, in every nightclub, who had shouted across all those restaurants, walked right by me in front of all my swell friends and *cut me dead* . . . as if he'd never seen me before in his life—never! He passed me by like so much white trash.

Of course, this man was in so big with the court because he was the *biggest* and the *mostest*. He had oil and everything that the empire was doing business with, and that was why he was given this *fantastic* position on the dais at court. That probably accounts for the jewel, too!

"Listen," I said to my English friends afterward, "you just don't know what your empire has to go through. King George and Queen Mary do. No flies on them! They know what's what! *This* is what makes the sun never set!"

As you can tell, I think of royalty as being a bit of all right.

Sorry to keep going on about Queen Mary, but I was crazy about her. I used to see her about three times a week in London because she loved these shops where I went. The old gent who owned one of the shops said, "There is a difference between you and Her Majesty the Queen, madam, if you don't mind my saying it. The difference is when you like something, you ask to buy it; but, you know, when Her Majesty comes in here, we lock up the best, because she expects everything for nothing." It was really hit and run with her; she just grabbed.

One day during my London years, I was buying something —I think china—in Goode's on South Audley Street. Goode's is the best-run shop in the world. At one point a salesman said, "Excuse me, madam, but Her Majesty is coming through. Perhaps you might step back for just a minute."

We were in a room of very cheap vases—glass vases. I don't know if you've ever been in Goode's, but it's made up of small rooms, so that you get lots of wall space for the stuff that they've got for sale. And so I stepped back.

She looked so queenly. This day she was in blue. Everything matched—including the pale blue fox to go with the pale blue tailleur and the pale blue kid laced boots. And the pale blue toque. I stepped back. And, my God! something on my coat or my sleeve— I had a big fur-lined tweed coat on—hit a glass vase, and each piece of glass on either side hit another piece of glass, and all this glass came shattering down. I was like a sort of crucifixion figure against the wall in the middle. It was . . . too . . . *horrible!* The Queen went by and looked at me as if to say, "Well, we *are* busy these days!" Yes, she went straight by without a comment, but she gave me very much of a smile. She probably thought I was a wonderful housekeeper, very busy with my little home.

She always wore matching clothes. The toque. You know the Queen Mary toque. Then the fox. Then the tailleur. Then the boots. All the same color: pale blue, pale lavender, sometimes cream color, sometimes white, pale green, pale rose. She only had one getup in each of those different colors.

So I said to my father, "Guess who I saw this afternoon— Queen Mary!" And I described her.

Father said, "Never could stand the *Tecks!* Bum lot!" Dismissed the whole family, who are German, you know, and went on to the next subject.

I thought she was wonderful. Simply wonderful! Had such a carriage. She must have been so tired—all those bazaars, you know, garden parties, and so forth. But I don't think it's so boring. You have everything you want; no one gets in your way; you get everything done, which is great; and you only do what you can, and you do a lot, and you *demand* a lot to do. I'd like to have been Elizabeth the First. She was *wonderful.* She surrounded herself with poets and writers, lived at Hampton Court, and drove that little team of spotted ponies with long tails. Their manes and tails were dyed the same color as her hair—you know royalty—*red*! She ruled little England and dreamt of empire! She's at the top of my list. I loved the clothes. It took her four hours to dress—we had a lot in common! No, I wouldn't mind being a public servant: well paid, well housed, beautifully treated. No, not at all. Suit me down to the ground.

CHAPTER
TEN

Did I tell you about the Duke of Windsor's bathroom at the Moulins? After lunch, the Duchess said to me, "Come upstairs. I want to show you something."

So there was the Duke's bathroom, not very big, say from there to here . . . but ample. The tub was covered over with a wooden board which he'd obviously had one of the men on the property make —a kind of table. It was piled with papers, papers . . . pa-pers, PAPERS! Bills, little things to do with golf. The Duchess said, "Isn't this terrible? Look at this heap!" Well, of course, she was right—nothing but a *mass* of papers. It's very English. What was so odd was that this mess was in the house of the best housekeeper in the world, where naturally everything, between dozens of housemaids, was perpetually organized every day. You might expect all sorts of things in such a house—but *not that table*! So we were roaring with laughter. The Duchess said, "What can I do? Look at this thing."

Suddenly the Duke appeared: "What are you two doing in here?! May I ask you two ladies to get the hell *out*! This happens to be *my* bathroom, and that happens to be *my* table."

So he kicked us both out of the bathroom. We hadn't touched a thing. We just gazed in horror. Yes, there was a shower right there in the bathroom, but it wasn't in the tub. Oh, I'm sure he used the shower. There was a glass door on it so the water wouldn't splash out on his papers. Oh, I'm sure he took showers. There was nothing unwashed about the Duke. My God! We know about the English, but I do think that he had his two a day.

I first met the Duke at the polo matches on Long Island when the Argentines were here in the twenties—the golden Prince of Wales, heir to the throne. "Did I do the right thing?" After he abdicated, the Duke must have asked himself that question every day of his life. It tormented the Duchess, too. One day I arrived in Paris. The Duchess called me on the telephone and said, "Oh, Diana, I know you've just arrived, but come out here and have dinner with me. I'm all alone." This was after the Duke had died. I went out to the house in Neuilly. The Duchess looked too beautiful, standing in the garden, dressed in a turquoise djellaba embroidered in black pearls and white pearls—marvelous—and wearing all her sapphires. She was so affectionate, a loving sort of friend—very rare, you know. Women are rarely that sort of friend to each other. Men are much more fond of each other. At least, that's what I *think*.

So we were talking after dinner, the two of us. And then suddenly she took hold of my wrist, gazed off into the distance, and said: "Diana, I keep telling him he must not abdicate. *He must not abdicate.* No, no, no! No, no, no, I say!" Then, suddenly, after this little mental journey back more than thirty-five years, her mind snapped back to the present; she looked back at me, and we went on talking as we had been before.

I first met her when I was running a little lingerie business near Berkeley Square. It was my first job. It was in a mews where a friend of mine kept his cars. Above the cars there was nothing doing, and that's where I started the shop and supervised all the work. I was always in Paris finding fabrics, finding designs. . . . We had some women who sewed in the shop, but the most beautiful work was done in a Spanish convent in London, and that's where I spent my time. There was a brief period in my life when I spent *all* my time in convents. I was never *not* on my way to see the mother superior for the afternoon. "I want it rolled!" I'd say. "I don't want it *hemmed*, I want it *r-r-r-rolled!*"

Ah! You don't know the *fabrics* we had! You don't know the *luxe*, you don't know the *beauty*. . . . I mean, someone like my friend Mona Williams would come in and spend five thousand dollars —this is on *bedsheets*—which, of course, was an enormous sum. She collected them. Laid them away in linen closets and chests. She treated them like the most beautiful French dresses. And then the *nightgowns* . . .

One day Wallis Simpson came into the shop. I didn't really know her then. I'd met her at a party at the embassy when we first arrived in London. She wasn't very well dressed then. She wasn't in what you'd call the smart set—at all. We didn't become great friends then. But one day she invited me to lunch and I went. And I've *never* eaten a meal like I had that day for lunch. All the people at the table that day said that they'd never had such a lunch. She gave other luncheons like this, always with the most remarkable food, and that's what really established her as a hostess in London, which she was by the time she walked into my shop.

She knew *exactly* what she wanted. She ordered three nightgowns, and this is what they were: First, there was one in white satin copied from Vionnet, all on the bias, that you just pulled down over your head. Then there was one I'd bought the original of in Paris from a marvelous Russian woman. All the great *lingères*, the workers of lingerie, were Russian, because they were the only people who really knew luxury when luxury was in fashion. The whole neck of this nightgown was made of petals, which was too extraordinary, because they were put in on the bias, and when you moved they rippled. Then the third nightgown was a wonderful crêpe de chine. Two were pale blue, another in white—three pieces in all.

By this time she had left her husband, Ernest Simpson. She was on her own then. She didn't have anyone to support her, so this was a big splurge for her. The nightgowns were for a very special weekend. The Prince of Wales had discovered Wallis Simpson.

She gave our shop three weeks to do the job. "This is the

date!" she said. "This is the deadline!" So then a week went by and she called again: "How are those nightgowns getting on?" Then, in the third week, she called every day.

She was on her way to her first weekend alone at Fort Belvedere with her Prince.

Then . . . suddenly, she had the most beautiful clothes in London and the most divine house in Great Cumberland Terrace, filled with white lilacs and burning perfume and the whole bit.

The other evening I dined with my oldest friend, Edwina d'Erlanger—just the two of us. After dinner we started talking about our life in London together during the thirties. "Oh, Edwina," I said, "didn't we love our Golden Prince of Wales!"

He *was* the Golden Prince. To say that now, after all these years . . . it sounds a little mawkish. But you must understand that to be a woman of my generation in London—*any* woman—was to be in love with the Prince of Wales.

That evening I told Edwina a story I'd told no one but Reed. The year must have been 1930, because I remember Reed was away in New York on business that year and I was home alone in London. One night a friend was going to take me to dinner and to a movie at a divine movie house on Curzon Street where you called up to reserve tickets and where everybody knew everybody—it was rather chic to go, but it was important to be on time. My friend was to pick me up at precisely eight o'clock.

Eight o'clock arrived. Then eight-fifteen. I was standing in front of the fire downstairs, wondering. I couldn't believe it, because my friend was always extremely prompt, as all Englishmen were in those days. Eight-thirty arrived, and I told Coglin, the butler, that I'd have my dinner on a tray. Coglin, who was an extraordinary man— he had a marvelous *correctness* about him—suggested that I wait another fifteen minutes.

At ten minutes to nine, in walked a man who hadn't shaved since morning, whose tie was askew, whose collar was rumpled. You simply didn't *see* men like that at ten to nine in the evening in London.

I'm not saying that he'd be in white tie, but he'd be clean as a whistle —and *on time*.

"Diana," he said, "I have just lived through the most terrible day of my life. At nine o'clock this morning I was called to Buckingham Palace to meet the King and the Prince of Wales. I sat in the room with them, lunch was served, a bottle of wine was passed . . . we made conversation—stiffly. Then . . ."

The man who was telling me all this is dead now. He was a charming, handsome man, named Fruity Metcalfe. He was the Prince of Wales's aide-de-camp; he was a polo player the Prince had picked up in India; he married Lord Curzon's youngest daughter, you know, Baba, Lady Alexander. He didn't do very much in life. I once asked him, "Fruity, what do you do in the morning?"

"I dress."

"Well, so do I."

"Well, they put out my ties and so forth and I have to *choose*."

In any case, he had been the Prince of Wales's aide-de-camp. The reason he was there for lunch with King George and the Prince was that the Prince insisted someone else be in the room with himself and King George, who was an absolutely terrifying man. The King never spoke in public except in the House of Lords, but when he did it was *blood* and *thunder*. . . .

So you can imagine what a dramatic moment it was when the Prince of Wales looked his father, the King, *straight* in the eye and told him that never, *under any circumstances*, would he succeed him.

This, you understand, was long before he had even met Wallis Simpson. It had nothing to do with giving up the throne for the woman he loved. Isn't that the damnedest story you ever heard? I didn't even tell Reed about it for five or six years. I was so afraid that if I said it out loud I'd get in the *habit* of saying it.

In retrospect, it all seems so logical. For one thing, the Prince of Wales was born a very modern man. I'm not sure he really believed in the monarchical system. Now I'm not talking about his love of country. That was overpowering.

Once, I arrived at Neuilly, outside of Paris, for quite a big dinner. I had on white satin slippers. There's never *been* such rain! I mean the rain was falling down and jumping up off the ground. The Duke was at the door, which I thought was terribly charming— you know, with the two footmen there—and he was just roaring with laughter as I was struggling out of the car. And I got in soaking, absolutely soaking, and I said, "Your country, sir!" meaning that it rained too much there in France, or certainly at that moment, and his whole countenance changed.

"*My* country?!" He . . . was . . . furious . . . at my suggesting that *France* was his country. Oh, he wasn't joking at all! Of course, immediately he recovered himself and was charming. But I had hit on something that was just about the . . . *end*.

Reed and I were no longer living in England by the time Edward became King and then abdicated. But my sister's brother-in-law, Lord Brownlow, was *very* much involved. He was Edward's lord-in-waiting. That meant that he could be called upon at any time of the day or night. Naturally, this rarely happened. He'd be invited for dinner, the way I'd invite you for dinner; the King didn't follow every move he made. Then, on the one day in history when the King really needed Lord Brownlow, he was nowhere to be found. *Finally,* they found him in a Turkish bath. He'd been on a bit of a toot, I guess, and he was having a good old massage when the message came through: Would he please go directly to Fort Belvedere, bringing a change of clothing?

When Perry got to the fort, the King told him *exactly* what was expected of him: He was to dine, and then, immediately after dinner, he was to leave with Mrs. Simpson and drive to Southampton, where they were to board the Channel boat as Mr. and Mrs. Something or other. That turned out to be a terrible mistake. Perry's face was known everywhere, because he'd been seen walking beside the King into Parliament, walking into White's, or wherever. And by this time you couldn't miss Wallis Simpson. She didn't dress any more exaggeratedly than I'm dressed at this moment, but there was something about her that made you look twice. Well, they were spotted, and the story got out that the two had boarded the boat, that they were crossing the Channel. . . .

Perry told Reed and me about this when we were visiting London about six weeks after the abdication. He called us late one night and said, "Please come to see Kitty and me."

So, still dressed for dinner, we arrived.

"I've been back two weeks," Perry told us when we got there. "This is my life: today I walk into White's and every man leaves the bar. I walk down Seymour Street, where Kitty and I have lived all these years, and if I see a friend he crosses to the other side of the street. Nobody—but *nobody*—speaks to me in London. It's as if people really believed I was a party to the abdication—to a conspiracy! Kitty doesn't want to listen to this. She'll go up to bed. But I will tell you and Reed *everything*."

Kitty did go up to bed, being totally exhausted at this point by the pressures of a world-shaking event in which her husband was more involved than anyone—except, of course, the King and Mrs. Simpson.

Perry went on. "We crossed the Channel, Wallis and I," he said, "and our first night was in Rouen, where we found rooms in a hotel, just like ordinary tourists on the road. 'Perry,' Wallis said to me through the door, after we'd been in our separate rooms for what seemed like an eternity, 'will you please leave the door open between your room and mine? I'm so frightened. I'm so nervous.' I did. Then she called to me: 'Perry, will you please sleep in the bed next to me? I cannot be alone.' "

So he went into her room, fully dressed, and pulled the blanket up over himself . . . and then, *suddenly*, she started to cry. "Sounds came out of her," Perry said, "that were absolutely without top, bottom . . . that were *primeval*. There was nothing I could do but lie down beside her, hold her hand, and make her *feel* that she was not alone."

The next morning, Perry told us, a call came through from

the King. The hotel was very simple, and Mrs. Simpson had to take the call at the concierge's desk. By this time the *whole* of Rouen knew who Wallis was. They were standing in the hall, in the street, in the square—*hundreds* of them—while Perry and the maid and the driver who were traveling with them tried to shield them so that she could have a little privacy in which to talk.

The next day they hit Cannes. There, the King would call two and three times a day. The lines were tapped so they could literally hear twenty clicks as they came on. "Is *everybody* listening?" Mrs. Simpson would say. "*Now* we're going to start to talk." That was the only way to handle it—to let people *know* that they knew that they were being listened to. And then Mrs. Simpson spoke to him: "You will never *ever* see me again. I will be lost in South America." Don't forget, South America was still a place you could get lost in in those days. "*Never* leave your country! You *cannot* give in! You can *not*! You were *born* to this, it is your *heritage*, it is *demanded* of you by your country, by the traditions of nine hundred years. . . ."

And et cetera.

Anyway, the King took absolutely no heed, and the abdication took place. Perry was called to Windsor from Cannes. He saw the farewells.

"Edward went up to Queen Mary," Perry told Reed and me, "and kissed her on both hands and then on both cheeks. She was as cold as ice. She just looked at him. Then he said goodbye to Prince Henry, Duke of Gloucester, and to Prince George, Duke of Kent, who both broke down in tears. Then he approached the new King, King George VI, who *completely* broke down. 'Buck up, Bertie!' the Duke said. 'God save the King!' And with that, he turned, walked away, and that was it."

Perry accompanied the Duke of Windsor on the battleship that took him to Calais. From there, the Duke went to Vienna, where he stayed in a castle that belonged to Eugène de Rothschild. Perry went to Cannes to see Mrs. Simpson and to bring news back to the Duke. He told us that he had arrived at about 6:00 a.m.—the sun was just coming up—and that he had been met by a footman who took him through this cold, lonely castle to a room. He went into the room and there he saw the Duke—who looked just like a little schoolboy, sound asleep, with sun coming across his blond hair. His bed was surrounded by chairs . . . and on each chair was a picture of his beloved Wallis.

"It was an obsession," Perry said. "No greater love has ever existed. I stayed there two days with him. Now I'm back in London, and this is my reward—I am completely, *totally* alone."

We never talked about it again, Perry and I. It obviously affected him very much. He must have paced five miles up and down as Reed and I listened to him. Reed and I never said one word. Perry was a charming, erudite gentleman who was forever tainted by being involved with a King at the wrong moment.

Do you know what time it was when Reed and I walked out into Seymour Street? Seven-thirty in the morning. It was *bright daylight*. That's why I remember what I had on: a beautiful dress, I think Chanel's—this was the thirties, so it must have been—of navy-blue crêpe de chine, and from the knees down it was white organdy. Reed was wearing a dinner jacket. Here we were, walking through the streets of Mayfair in the early morning . . . dressed absolutely to the *nines*.

CHAPTER ELEVEN

I never discuss politics—they're beyond my ken. But I do know that the rise of Hitler—which more or less coincided with the abdication of the Duke—was the passing of the empire.

Several years ago, right after *The Damned* was released, I had dinner with Luchino Visconti in Rome. I told him that a part of the Night of the Long Knives—which he does so marvelously in *The Damned*—had actually taken place on three floors above me in the Vier Jahreszeiten Hotel in Munich.

Reed and I had been down in the lovely Swan Country—the valley below Munich—that day, and we returned to the hotel in the early evening in a terrific hurry to change our clothes and get to a concert. At first, all we could make out was this tremendous agitation in front of the hotel—cars, cars, *cars*—huge Mercedes-Benzes with the great silver pipes on the outside, tops down so that the populace could see the grandeur of the people they carried—the captains of Hitler's new order. Out of the cars emerged Röhm's officers, with spiked helmets, swords jangling, and overcoats to the ground. Everything was metallic. Just sticking out from beneath their long coats were spurs—though, of course, they got about as close to a horse as you and I are right now. In the street, a regiment of goose-stepping soldiers went by—the clap, clap, clap of their leather boots as they hit the pavement—and they were shouting, "*Heil! Heil! Heil!*" but to the *heavens*!

I pushed my way past all of this, into the hotel, to get up into my bath. "Really," Reed said to me, "you've got to behave yourself. You simply cannot push your way past these men saying, 'Excuse me, excuse me, I've got to get to my bath!' You've got to realize that you are in somebody else's country and it's been taken over by this special breed of people."

We got through that evening all right. Actually, we were having the time of our lives. Every day we went out into the lovely, sweet-smelling countryside—which was quite untouched then—having picnics and revisiting the castles of mad King Ludwig, which we could never see enough of.

This is the tour: First you go to Nymphenburg. Ludwig was born there. You get a little bit of *early* Wagner here.

Then . . . you go to Neuschwanstein. You leave your car, get in a carriage, and then eventually you have to walk, because it's really on a mountain peak. Inside, it's all *Tannhäuser*—all of it—and the outside is so beautiful, with these towers like candles on the top of the mountain. It's a child's dream of a castle. There is no countryside like the Swan Country was then. Grass waist-high, turrets everywhere, the sky blue.

Then—these are the steps of Ludwig's life—the next stop is Linderhof, which is divine—it's the most perfect example of kitsch in the history of the world. You see a huge gold throne at the head of a dining table. There, draped in ermine tails, Ludwig would dine with the busts of . . . Louis XIV and Madame de Maintenon or Louis XV and Madame de Pompadour or whatever combination struck his fancy on that particular night. Their busts were set on chairs. The table came up through a hole in the floor with the meal on it so that *they* never had to see a servant. The meal would come up; they'd eat; they'd of course enjoy the conversation, the mad Ludwig and his busts —*tous les trois* or *tous les* whatever, and then, at midnight, he'd leave them and go outside. Every time he'd pass a statue of Marie Antoinette in the gardens he'd sweep off his hat and bow. They were all royal, of course. Then he'd wander over the countryside because he couldn't sleep. There's a marvelous painting I once saw of Ludwig alone on a small sleigh pulled by eight peacocks—two by two by two by two. I don't think that Ludwig actually did this—whoever painted it was probably madder than he was—but it's a pretty idea.

Also, at Linderhof there's a small door you go through and you're in the Blue Grotto! There is this extraordinary *aura* of light, and there Ludwig would float on the water in a golden seashell of a boat, while from a balcony within the grotto an orchestra performed everything they knew of Wagner for hour after hour after *hour*. . . .

Then . . . there's Herrenchiemsee, where he's getting into a more "classical" period, shall we say—and it's the *end*. . . . He tried to build something finer, larger, and more splendid than Versailles. He was totally gone by then, having had so many talks at dinner with those marble statues.

I think it was Goethe who said, "There is a glory to madness that only madmen know." It's a beautiful statement, but I'm afraid I may have made it up. If I did, it's better than his.

These were our days around Munich. Then we'd go back to the Vier Jahreszeiten in the early evening, and at night we'd hear some music, which was always remarkable—the best music in the world is in Germany, after all. The stars would come out, we'd listen to this music . . . our life was a dream of beauty.

But the contrast of this beauty with the absurdity of those comic-opera bullies we encountered. . . .

One morning, Julie, my maid from London, came in late with the breakfast, shivering, shaking, and weeping. She said, "Madam, madam, madam . . . we must leave today."

"What do you mean, 'leave today'?" I said. "We've got another four days here, and you know it—and you love Munich."

"Madam, *please* . . . something terrible is happening in this hotel!"

"Well, if it's *that* terrible, couldn't you tell me what it is?"

"That's just it—I don't know what it is! But I know that

when I leave this room—I've been twice to this floor this morning trying to bring you your breakfast—everything's delayed. Something's happening on the three floors above you. Something's going on up there."

"Listen, Julie, there's nothing to get upset about as long as you can get from your room to—"

"Oh, madam, madam . . ."

"Listen, Julie, cheer up and let's get on with it!"

So she got me dressed and out and everything seemed normal enough. But Julie was getting more and more upset until she couldn't even fasten a hook. She was a very sensible Frenchwoman, nothing simpering about her. She knew she was in very, very bad company.

Then we returned to London. Ten days later, *The Times* gave an account of the fourteen murders that had been committed that night upstairs at the Vier Jahreszeiten! It was the Night of the Röhm Murders—the Night of the Long Knives, which took place all over the country.

I've learned a tremendous amount from maids in my life.

Do you remember the scene in *The Damned* of officers in women's underwear? Elsie Mendl showed me photographs of exactly the same thing going on at her house—pictures that had been snapped by her wonderful old caretaker and his wife. They managed the gate lodge of her little house at Versailles, the Villa Trianon, and they stayed on when the Germans occupied the house.

First, you must imagine the beauty of Elsie's house. It had belonged to one of the members of the court of Louis Philippe, and there was something in the lease that gave her permission to open a door and walk right into the park at Versailles—the palace grounds that no one sees, way, way beyond all the canals and the formal gardens, farther away than the eye can see. You opened the gate of Elsie's little *potager*—her vegetable garden—and there you were under the big live oaks that had been there since the Kings of France. The live oaks were spaced very far apart, and there were sheep grazing underneath. It was like stepping into the eighteenth century.

Now imagine, if you can, the German officers, so obscene with their helmets and their mustaches, running around in this garden in Elsie's underclothes! Somehow or other, the caretaker and his wife found the ways and means of taking the pictures—the officers were too drunk to notice, I suppose. There weren't many of them, but *those*, I can tell you, were some *pictures*.

CHAPTER
TWELVE

Let's suppose you were a total stranger—*and* a very good friend. That's a good combination. What would you want to know about me? And how would you go about *finding* it out?

To me, the books I've read are the giveaway. My life has been more influenced by books than by any other one thing. I stopped reading—*seriously* reading—years ago. But what I read before then has remained forever secure in my mind, because I used to read and reread and *reread*. The real seriousness of my youth—by which I mean my young married years—was that I devoted myself totally to learning. From the time I got married at eighteen until the time I went to work in 1937, twelve years—I read. And Reed and I would read things together out loud, which was *marvelous*. That was the charm of it—when you've *heard* the word, it means so much more than if you've only seen it.

Reed and I had seven thousand books, between our own and the boys', that we had to sell when we sold the house in Brewster. It was cash on delivery, because it was a house that was not easily sold. Our lives in the city were too full to properly use the house and its garden. It was on three levels, which is what made it hard to sell, but that's also what made it so romantic. When we decided to sell it, it was one of those things you don't think about. It was done. And these awful people would come and they'd say, "Now what *period* would you call this?"

"Well, it's many periods," I'd say, "many thoughts. . . ."

It was far and away the most romantic country house you could ever imagine. The top of my bed was over twenty feet high— *à la polonaise*. And I had every door inside painted a different color— pale lavender, pale blue, pink, strong yellow—I had such a color sense in those days. But we rarely went there. I suppose that's why we sold it. You see, I've always been a gypsy. I mean, by the time we lived there I'd lived in Europe and then America and then Europe and then America *again*. I can never have the feeling other people have about their roots, their own soil, as I remember telling Reed when we sold the house. I have no sense of soil—at all. But for the same reason, it was mad to sell the books.

There've been several constants in my reading from the start. The Russians were the first.

Tolstoy! Tolstoy, naturally, was always my favorite. And when I think of Natasha in *War and Peace*, when she's just seen a young lady kiss a young man she was obviously having a walkout with and then she sees a young lieutenant and she follows him into the conservatory and she *grabs* his hand . . . I know *exactly* what she was wearing. It's actually known as the "Natasha dress." Where would fashion *be* without literature?

Japan was another constant. *The Tale of Genji* and *The Pillow Book* of Sei Shonagon have been Japan to me since I first read them and reread them in Albany and in Regent's Park. This is my cult. Some people have their Proust; I have my *Pillow Book*. I still keep it next to my bed. Meanderings of the mind, very charming. Little vignettes of wisdom and beauty.

I met Arthur Waley, the translator of *Genji* and *The Pillow Book*, in London. He was the handsomest man. And his translations of Chinese poetry are exquisite: "The birds are flying high, the swallows are flying low, knowing that it's going to rain. . . ." Just three or four lines. This is my paraphrase, you understand, not the *poetry* . . . which is *to die*.

It was Chips Channon's book on the Wittelsbachs, *The Ludwigs of Bavaria*, that got me going on my Bavarian and Hungarian kicks. This was all in Regent's Park and on rainy weekends in the country in England. I'd spend days and *days* in bed reading and think nothing of it. But there were so *many* books. I learned *everything* in England. I learned *English*.

Maybe it's because I've been such a gypsy that I associate my reading so closely with the houses I was living in at the time. But, curiously enough, the hours of reading I remember most vividly are the months we stayed in Switzerland at the Hôtel Beau-Rivage when we'd left London but before we moved to New York. The boys were at school just down the lake, and every afternoon they would come for tea. We had a big sitting room with a fire and a huge table covered with jams and eggs, which the boys would eat, and then Reed and I would go downstairs for our dinner. But before then Reed, in this marvelous, *sustained* voice he had—he was a singer, you see—would read to them from Hans Christian Andersen and from Chinese fairy tales and from Russian fairy tales—out loud: It's midnight, and the white polar bear is carrying the Princess to see the man she loves the most, and that's all that's on her mind, and she really *is* a Princess. And the polar bear is white, and the ice is blue, and the sky is *midnight* blue. . . .

I was so happy in Ouchy, on the water. My bed faced Mont Blanc. Every night, I'd leave a small space open between the curtains so that I could see Mont Blanc in the morning when I woke up. And some mornings—this was in the winter, when the snow lay very, *very* thick on it—it would have a pink glaze. Other mornings it would have a blue glaze to it. I would sit and watch the pinks and blues change during the day as the light changed and the clouds constantly moved across the sky. Every day was totally and completely different. I can remember thinking how much like my own temperament it was—how much like everyone's temperament. The light on Mont Blanc was a revelation of what we all consist of. I mean, the shadows and the colors and the ups and the downs and the wonderment . . . it was like our growing up in the world.

I think people forget that I have a family. In London people never thought of me as having any children. They thought I was only involved with clothes—and I *was*. But the family was *very* close. And though I did think terrifically about my sons, I wasn't that close to them. I had an English nanny by then and the best French nursery-maid in London, so they were always speaking French. For them it was a very conventional upbringing of the period—up to a point.

Wednesday was the nurse's day off, and also the nursery-maid's, and that was my afternoon with my sons. If the weather was good, I'd take them across the street to the zoo in Regent's Park with its ducks and flowers. Timmy and Frecky would go *straight* to their friends the gorillas. The boys knew the keeper, so we'd go into their quarters behind the cage and he'd bring in the gorillas. He'd leave us *alone* with these three *enormous* gorillas . . . and no cage! I had made a solemn vow to myself never to allow my children to know that anything in the world was frightening, impure, or impossible. Therefore, the gorillas were *divine*, and I had to sit and admire the slaps and pats they gave my two miniature sons. My boys would sit there with their arms around them, kissing them from time to time . . . they were no more frightened of those gorillas than they would be of you.

Then . . . if it was *really* raining, we'd go to Madame Tussaud's Wax Museum and see the beheadings. That was a bit of all right for them. Nothing wrong for them to see. Everybody had to *go*! All I can say is that my sons had a very healthy upbringing. And they've gone through life the same way. They've never been afraid of anything . . . physical or strange or bizarre.

On the walls of each of their rooms—they had separate rooms, which is *very* important—I put maps of the world. Then, when Reed and I would go abroad for several days to some delicious place like Tunisia or into the long grass of Bavaria, I'd show them exactly where we were going. It's not that they were that interested in where we were going . . . but they'd connect the *place* with the *idea*. They never grew up with a provincial point of view.

People such as myself who've had no education are hungry . . . reaching out for something, as long as they don't have to do it in a schoolroom with a gong going all the time. But I was determined my children wouldn't be brought up that way.

In London we sent them to Mr. Gibbs's school, which was very good and very conventional. They learned to read and write before they were four or five, which is *essential*—all children should. "Give me a child for seven years . . ." as the Jesuits say.

When Timmy was eight, we sent him to school in Switzerland. I hated doing it. But we didn't keep them in London, because in those days the only boys who didn't go away to boarding school were tubercular or something.

After we moved to America, the boys' education didn't cost us much. They both went through Groton on scholarships. I said, "Your *father* works, your *mother* works. . . ." Nothing like a good push!

In many ways, I was a very conventional parent, though perhaps I never *looked* like a conventional parent. I can remember visiting the boys at Groton. Naturally, I was dressed to kill, and as rouged as I am now—if not *more*. The first little boy I saw said, "How do you do, Mrs. Vreeland?"

"How do you do?" I said. "But tell me, how did you know I was Mrs. Vreeland?"

"Because," he said, "Timmy and Frecky said, 'If you see a woman with red ears—that's our mother!' "

I don't think it bothered them. Eventually you learn to live with your parents. In London, in the days when people used to play parlor games, we played a game where you'd choose your parents. Once, I remember, someone decided to be very clever and chose Mussolini and Emerald Cunard. Well, the place broke up into such a *row* . . . I never even got my turn. But I can remember saying, "Do you know what you'd be with parents like that? You'd be the smallest coin at the bottom of the basin!"

I didn't have a clever answer ready for myself. If I'd had the chance, I knew that I'd have chosen my parents *exactly* as they were.

And I had splendid godparents. Wouldn't change them for the world! I've told you about Baby Belle Hunnewell. Bob Chanler was my godfather—Uncle Bob. He painted. That's a lovely screen of his out in the front hall. He was a great big man with huge gray curls always filled with paint—gold and silver. He often came to our house with green hair and wild spirits and shouted up at us. Mad for girls and all that. My father was best man at one of his weddings. He was very much of the Diaghilev school of "Let's-go-all-the-way-all-the-time!" He had a beautiful house on Nineteenth Street.

Bob Chanler once said, "Send the children down. They can have lunch here. They can walk around the garden." So we arrived. No one answered the bell. Bong! We could hear it ringing inside the house. No one answered. Finally the door opened a crack. It was a Chinese cook. He said, identifying himself, "Mr. Bob's cook! Mr. Bob's cook!" He looked terrified. He kept saying "Big, big, big, big!" and spreading his hands as if he were showing us a monstrous-sized fish. It turned out there was a large boa constrictor loose in the house. Something had gone wrong the night before, and the boa constrictor was roaming around and no one could find it. We left immediately. We never discovered if Bob Chanler was loose in there too. No, I think it was just this Chinese chef and the boa constrictor.

My other godfather was Henry Clews. He always had wives who were great beauties and great ladies. When he came to dinner he had to sit in a rocking chair, because that was his style. He simply didn't like a straight-backed chair. Sometimes, if he felt like it, he wore his hat to the table—a beautiful, loose, floppy black fedora.

He was my father's best friend in the world. My father hadn't seen him in, say, thirty-five years, and so in his late eighties he decided to cross the big pond, the Atlantic, to see his old friend in La Napoule in the south of France.

My father arrived early in the morning on the Riviera, but he wasn't met. He managed to get to this magnificent castle out on a neck of land that stuck out into the Mediterranean. He was told: "His Majesty will see you at quarter to three, Mr. Dalziel." It took about four of these announcements to get my father into the mood that he was in the hands of madness—which he didn't like. He didn't have a thing to do. He walked in the gardens. He smoked cigarettes. He went up to his room two or three times. Then he came down. Finally a servant approached him—probably a very reliable sort—and said, "Would you come, sir, to the throne room, where Their Majesties will receive you."

So my poor darling Daddy went to the "throne room" . . . I mean, like a child is taken to the leopard house or something. And there were the two of them on their thrones—dressed to the nines, crowns and everything—and Mrs. Clews came down off the dais: "Fred! How wonderful to receive you. This is such a pleasure for Henry and myself. Please sit down. We're going to have a little lunch in a few minutes."

My father had consumed about four breakfasts by this time. He was not amused. He was not amused *at all*! He asked to have a car, and he left for Paris before dinner. He couldn't go through with it. He was too old to fool around with. He came back and said to me, "You see, my dear Diana, if Henry had said, 'Look, I've got the biggest spoof on the whole Riviera. Got this magnificent castle . . . and we're having the time of our lives. Most people our age don't have the time of their lives, but we're having it! Join us!' "—that might have been all right. Instead of that, he played his spoof *off* my father, his best friend. No, my father was not amused; he was terribly hurt. And when he told me this, his eyes flooded with tears. Because, naturally, when you're almost ninety, you've lost all your friends, no? I'd say he was eighty-nine or ninety then. Oh, it's such a sad story. And it was so sweet.

CHAPTER
THIRTEEN

God, taxis are expensive! I should take a bus like the rest of the world. You can't picture it? Neither can my grandchildren. They tell a story about me: "Nonnina"—that's what they call me; it's Italian for "little grandmother"—"Nonnina took a bus with Grandpa once, and you know what she said to him? 'Oh, look! There are other *people* here!' "

Every time I *have* taken a bus, which naturally is about three or four times, I've had to ask the driver what the fare is. Naturally, the whole bus breaks into laughter. They go to pieces. So to explain, I say, "You see, I'm not from your country. I'm . . . Chinese!"

Don't think I was always like this. When I went to work, I behaved like everyone else. I could use the *subway*.

Not long after we arrived back in New York in 1937, I was asked to work. I'd just arrived. I'd only been here for six months and I was going through money like one goes through . . . a bottle of scotch, I suppose, if you're an alcoholic. You couldn't keep any money *at all* in New York; it was so expensive after London. Carmel Snow, who was the editor of *Harper's Bazaar*, had seen me dancing at the St. Regis one night, and the next morning she called me up. She said she'd admired what I had on—it was a white lace Chanel dress with a bolero, and I had roses in my hair—and she asked me if I'd like a job.

"But Mrs. Snow," I said, "except for my little lingerie shop in London, I've never worked. I've never been in an office in my life. I'm never dressed until lunch."

"But you seem to know a lot about clothes," Carmel said.

"That I do. I've dedicated hours and *hours* of very detailed time to my clothes."

"All right, then why don't you just try it and see how it works out?"

I knew so little when I started. I must have terrified them. One of those early days at *Harper's Bazaar* I had a brainwave! I had on slacks like this and a little Chanel shirt with pockets inside, not on the outside like pockets are today. I said to an editor ambling around the hall, "I've got the best idea!" I took him into my office. "We're going to eliminate all handbags."

"You're going to *what*?"

"Eliminate all handbags. Now look. What have I got here? I carry much more than most people. I've got cigarettes. I've got my lipstick, I've got my comb, I've got my powder, I've got my rouge, I've got my money. But what do I want with a bloody old handbag that one leaves in taxis and so on? It should all go into pockets. Real pockets, like a man has, for goodness sake. Put the money here, lipstick and powder there, the comb and rouge here. Of course, you'd have much bigger pockets, and they'd be rather chic."

I told him how I would do the whole magazine just showing what you can do with pockets and how the silhouette is improved and so on, and also one's walk—there's nothing that limits a woman's walk like a pocketbook.

Well, the man ran from my office the way you run for the police! He rushed into Carmel's office and said, "Diana's going crazy! Get hold of her."

So Carmel came down and said, "Listen, Diana, I think you've lost your mind. Do you realize that our income from handbag advertising is God knows how many millions a year?!"

Well, she was correct, of course. It's the same as if they cut out men's *ties*. The country'd be destitute. "It's your birthday, I'm bringing a tie." The man who runs your building, what do you give him? A tie. It's your father's birthday, what do you give him? You give him a tie.

So I began that job. My father never referred to the fact that I worked for *Harper's Bazaar* because, of course, it was a *Hearst* publication. It wasn't that he objected to a woman working; it was that he hated the yellow press with *such* a passion. When I was growing up, no copies of any Hearst papers were allowed in the house. If a maid had been caught reading the *Daily Mirror*, she would have been fired. Oh, yes. And after I went to work, he never asked me how I was getting along, or how much money I was making, or whether they treated me well . . . the subject was never referred to—*ever*—because of his disapproval. And as for the fact that I was a great friend of Millicent Hearst's and her sons . . . the subject simply didn't exist for him.

Millicent died just a few years ago. I'm not big on funerals. I wouldn't bring this up if it were in the least macabre, but it's true: laid out in her coffin, she looked so absolutely ecstatic! She looked exactly like she did when she was the Belle of New York with every chandelier lit and all the bands playing. Really splendid. She looked . . . I mean, it was incredible! I've always been very fond of the Hearst boys, because I worked more than twenty-eight years for the Hearsts. Not that I had anything to do with the boys in terms of business—they didn't know what side was up in the magazines. But I have a great fondness for them. So I walked around the corner of Sixty-seventh Street to Millicent's apartment, and at the door Bill Hearst said, "You've got to see Mom. I'm sure this isn't up your alley at all, but you've *got* to see!" He said, "It's the goddamnedest thing!"

So we went into the dining room. It's always in the dining room they put these poor people! And I mean, it was the work of art of all artistry. I've never seen anything so amazing in my life. She was in the coffin, all set to *go*.

I only believe in cremation—fast, fast cremation. Done with. But Millicent Hearst really did look simply radiant!

Millicent gave the last big parties in New York that were any fun. When I first knew her, she lived on Riverside Drive in a castle. You walked in . . . and there were suits of shining armor everywhere. It was a great old-fashioned baronial hall, and Millicent would be standing in the center of it all, *roaring* with laughter. One night she'd wear emerald shoulder straps. Then the next night she'd wear diamond shoulder straps. And don't forget the emeralds and the diamons were *this* big, all across rather big shoulders. She was never a small girl—everything in a big way!

And *funny*! If she was going to make a joke, she'd start laughing, so she got you laughing before the joke was made, and by the time the joke *was* made, everybody was hysterical. She had quite an inflection. Instead of "the oil of Texas" and "the Earl of Sefton," shall we say, she'd say "the Oil of Sefton" and "the earl of Texas." She was from Brooklyn, and it was Brooklyn *all the way*. She was always surrounded by important, intelligent men. In London, in Paris, everywhere she went, she was treated like a great personality from this country. American royalty. And she never, never improved her English, nor did she care about it, nor did she know she was talking it— she didn't *hear* it. She was a hearty, lusty, wonderful *blonde* from *Brooklyn* who went all the way around the world *twice*. I think she was just plain too big for old William Randolph Hearst. And that was the reason for Marion Davies.

She was *another* fascinator. She was like Nell Gwynn—she had sold oranges in the street and now she slept with a king. She was the most delightful, provocative, amusing company—an alive, electric creature of total charm . . . and *power*. She wasn't all that different from Millicent. They both had power.

In New York the old boy never came down from the top of the Ritz Towers—apparently there were always creditors downstairs. But I often went *up* to see Marion. By this time, she'd lost a lot of her looks—she had one of those champagne chins which you don't see much anymore, because people have nips and lifts. She was a woman of great character—tremendously protective of W. R. He'd always said, "People with brain power never die. George Bernard Shaw and I will never die." When Shaw did die, Hearst was old and dying himself. That morning, Marion had the news cut out of all his newspapers that came in from the West—Hearst only read his papers from west of the Mississippi—so that he never read about Shaw's death.

Once Marion asked me if I had my breakfast in bed. I told her I did. "Oh, I wish I could," she said. "It must be so nice. I have to get up right away."

"Why?"

"Because . . ." she said, "he says it brings *mice.*"

So the day the old boy died, in my mind's eye I saw Marion sitting in a pretty bedjacket in her pretty bed in her hotel suite, eating a leisurely breakfast . . . *surrounded* by tiny mice! It's never left my imagination. I still see it *so* clearly.

I never met the old boy. But once, when I'd just started writing "Why Don't You?" for *Harper's Bazaar,* he sent me a note in his own hand: "Dear Miss Vreeland, It is always a pleasure to read your columns. I reread them all the time. I am a particular admirer of yours." I was so touched. Don't you love the "Miss"? He never dictated a letter, you see. He was an old-fashioned gentleman—in the sense that royalty never had anything typed.

That column "Why Don't You" first appeared in *Harper's Bazaar* in the summer of 1936. It was rather frivolous. I don't remember too many of the ideas, thank *goodness.* "For a coat to put on after skiing, get yourself an Italian driver's, of red-orange lined in dark green." That was one of them. "Have a furry elk-kid trunk for the back of your car." They were all very tried and true ideas, mind you. We had a trunk like that on the back of our Bugatti. "Knit yourself a little skullcap. Turn your old ermine coat into a bathrobe." The one that seemed to cause the most attention was the one about dead champagne. "Wash your blond child's hair in dead champagne, as they do in France." That even got S. J. Perelman stirred up. He wrote a very funny parody in *The New Yorker.* Carmel Snow wrote

Perelman a letter saying he shouldn't do such things, that it was very upsetting to such a young girl to be criticized! Good heavens! I was in my thirties at the time and was very flattered.

At first nobody gave me ideas for the column, but then they said to me, oh, put in your column that Daisy Fellowes's daughter drove away from the church in Paris in a two-in-hand. Well, I would have none of it, and besides, war was declared, which, thank God, put an end to the whole absurdity anyway.

But it was nice to know that old W. R. enjoyed them.

I never went to San Simeon when he was there. His son Bill often asked Reed and me, but for some reason or another we never went. One day, long after his father's death, Bill called from San Francisco and told us that it was our last chance to visit San Simeon as private guests. So we went. I remember calling the night before to say, "Be sure to have the zebras out."

Bill Hearst said, "Zebras. Good God, we haven't seen zebras around here in ten years!"

I said, "I'm coming for the *zebras*; I'm not coming for anything else."

You won't believe this—we arrived and there they were, this whole row, all the way up the two miles of the driveway into the mountains. Bill Hearst had probably forgotten he even *owned* zebras. We stayed about two and a half weeks, and we didn't see another sign of the zebras. And then, the morning we left to go to San Francisco, every zebra was back out to say goodbye, lining the road. Bill Hearst was astonished. I took it very personally. They had come out for me.

San Simeon was delightful—an extraordinary place. "But it's so vulgar," my friends said to me at the time. "How can you say it's extraordinary?"

"Because it's a man's dream," I said. "It's a particularly American dream. And that dream of W. R.'s came true. And in *that* way it *is* splendid."

San Simeon was not built for Millicent or Marion. Oh, no

—it was built for W. R. himself. Think of it: acres of roses, going for miles. A man's castle. Richelieu's bed. There was only a trace of the woman's touch there—barrels of bleach in the hairdressing department.

I believe women are naturally dependent on men. One admires and expects things from men that one doesn't expect from women, and such has been the history of the world. The beauty of painting, of literature, of music, of *love* . . . this is what men have given the world, not women.

As you can tell, you're not exactly talking to a feminist. I stand with the French line—woman and children last.

CHAPTER FOURTEEN

Do you realize how many times a week I hear about the thirties? Hardly a day goes by when someone doesn't say to me about something, "Oh, you'll love it, Mrs. Vreeland—it's so thirties." It's always déjà vu to me, but then a lot of things are. The point is that it was déjà vu to me *then*.

You never learned anything in the thirties. That's a terrible thing I've never said out loud to anyone before. But don't forget, we were going into the most appalling war in history, and you felt it in everything. Everything was weakening . . . I knew that we were heading toward *rien*.

Still, I loved the clothes I had in the thirties. I can remember a dress I had of Schiaparelli's that had fake ba-zooms—these funny little things that stuck out here. When you sat down, they sort of went . . . all I can say is that it was terribly chic. Don't ask me why, but it was. Another of my Schiaparellis that sticks in my mind was a black sheath with a long train in the form of a padded fishtail—I gave it to Gypsy Rose Lee, and she performed in it at the World's Fair —stalking the runway six times a day.

I loved my clothes from Chanel. Everyone thinks of *suits* when they think of Chanel. That came later. If you could have seen my clothes from Chanel in the thirties—the *dégagé* gypsy skirts, the divine brocades, the little boleros, the roses in the hair, the pailletted nose *veils*—day and evening! And the ribbons were so pretty.

I remember my great friend Leo d'Erlanger saying to me in Paris, "Diana, I want to give you a present. I know that what you love more than anything in the world is clothes, and I know that you love Chanel's clothes more than anyone else's. So I want you to go to Chanel and buy *anything* you want."

So I went to Chanel on the rue Cambon and I said to my *vendeuse*—the *vendeuse* is a kind of maître d'hôtel in a *maison de couture*—"Perhaps I'll buy something a bit more . . . mmm . . . *luxurious* then I usually do."

This was the dress I ordered: The huge skirt was of silver lamé, quilted in pearls, which gave it a marvelous weight; then the bolero was lace entirely encrusted with pearls and *diamanté*; then, underneath the bolero was the most beautiful shirt of linen lace. I think it was the most beautiful dress I've ever owned. I don't think I've ever been more grateful for a present.

Then the war came.

Reed and I had been in Capri, and on the way back from Capri we'd stopped in Paris. My husband was a man with such a marvelous sense of . . . how women are. He got on a ship with a lot of American friends leaving France, and he left me behind.

"You mean you'd leave your *wife*," they said—you know, that bourgeois spirit—"in a country that's at *war*?"

"Look," he said, "there's no point in taking Diana away from Chanel and her shoes. If she hasn't got her shoes and her clothes, there's no point in bringing her home. That's how it's always been and that's how it has to be."

I stayed on alone at the hotel—the Bristol, which was quite new then—for about two weeks. It was very quiet. The Phony War. Then, one morning, Leo d'Erlanger arrived there from London. "Diana," he said, "tomorrow afternoon at four o'clock you must leave. I've got you a place on a train, and it will take you to Le Havre, where I've got a cabin on a ship that will take you to New York. You've got to get out of France, you've got to get out of Europe—this is your last chance. It's the last passenger ship with private cabins out of Europe. This was my promise to Reed—when the time came to go, I'd get you out."

I'll never forget that afternoon, coming down the rue Cambon—my last afternoon in Paris for five years. I'd just had my last fitting at Chanel. I don't think I could have made it to the end of the block, I was so depressed—leaving Chanel, leaving Europe, leaving all the world of . . . of my world.

And then I saw this type coming up next to the Ritz, and it was my friend Ray Goetz, the most amusing man who ever lived. He had on a blue felt hat. He was married to Irene Bordoni. He was *big* in the theatre. He brought over that divine Spanish singer Raquel Meuller, who sang "Who Will Buy My Violets?" And that afternoon he could have taken me in his arms and looked after me for the rest of his life—not that he knew it.

"Oh, Ray!" I said. "Isn't it awful about the war?"

He turned. He looked at me for just a minute—just a split second—and asked, "What war?" And with that, he walked right past me, like a shadow.

How strange . . . it's always the same. Anyone can knock you over with a remark—or they can set you right up, which is what he did. I don't think I've ever been more grateful to a human being.

It was September. The days were getting shorter. It would be getting dark by six. That evening I remember walking up and down the Champs-Elysées with Johnny Faucigny-Lucinge. The weather was balmy, it was quite crowded with people, and it was *absolutely* quiet. I can remember exactly what I had on: a little black moiré tailleur from Chanel, a little piece of black lace wrapped around my head, and beautiful, absolutely exquisite black slippers like kid gloves . . . it's curious to visualize yourself like this, isn't it? But I always have to think about what I had on. Just today, I thought of those slippers and I remembered everything.

How long is the Champs-Elysées? At least a mile, wouldn't you say? We must have walked ten miles that night. All the tables were taken up from the sidewalks. There were no bands playing the "Marseillaise"—there was nothing. One hardly spoke. There was only this unearthly silence of hundreds of people strolling out of doors under the stars.

I asked Johnny to come up to my room at the Bristol for a last drink. In those days, I always traveled with a *nécessaire*. Oh, it was so beautiful—made to order, naturally—and inside was a little fitted crystal carafe, in which I always kept some brandy. Everyone traveled with a little brandy, because you were so often in railroad stations, where you could get waylaid in the rain and the snow and the cold and the damp, waiting for trains.

So when we got up to the room, exhausted—but this was *deep* exhaustion, not just physical exhaustion—I opened the *nécessaire*, took out the carafe with this brown liquid in it, opened it, and poured it into one bathroom glass for Johnny and then into another bathroom glass for myself—we didn't ring for glasses, because by this time it was very late. I brought the glass to my lips . . . and it wasn't brandy. Someone had emptied out the carafe and refilled it. It was tea—cold tea!

It was a heartbreaker. It was so letting down. I think it was the single most anticlimactic moment of my life. Cold tea!

CHAPTER

FIFTEEN

What amazing attitudes those marvelous people the English can conjure up! Especially when they're in trouble. Think of the Marquess of Bath, who owned Longleat. He went through the whole war with a duck on a lead, praying for bombs to fall so that his duck would have a pond to swim in.

Henry Bath was about as far as you can go in appeal—certainly for an Englishman. He had a lovely nose. He broke it breaking a bronc in Texas when he was very young, but a beautiful nose it remained. He joined the American forces—did you know that? Hank the Yank. Sort of like joining another table at El Morocco. He'd be asked, "Why are you here with the Americans?" and he answered, "Well, don't think I don't like the British—I mean, I *am* English." And he *was* too. He was quite somebody. As Marquess of Bath he wasn't some alley cat. He always had that duck, looking skyward, the two of them, and if they heard the *crunch* of a nearby bomb, they would set off on the dead run to see if the bomb crater would fill up with water so the duck could swim.

The British bat their best friends in the face, but that's all right because their friends can *take* it. Very tough society, the English.

Of course, it's only if you're both English that you can dish out this kind of behavior. An Englishman would take *great* exception if an American said something insulting to another Englishman. The English never let each other down. They'd never quite say, "Shut up!" —much too polite for that—but they'd say, "My dear sir . . ." quite slowly, and go on in that department and put you right on your *back*.

Ah, the Englishness of the English! The cold feet of the English! The kind hearts of the English! And never mind the bad teeth of the English!

In 1926, before we lived in London, we'd come over to England for a visit. Now London in 1926 was a big, good-natured town—it ran the world, don't forget. There wasn't the mixture of blood and nationalities that London has today and which I find terribly exciting. In those days, you were either a Cockney or you were a West Ender—period. And then suddenly the whole country went on strike. The General Strike. Do you realize *nothing* worked? There were no trains, there were no taxis, there were no telephones, there were no cables, there were no newspapers, there was no food— there was absolutely nothing. *Everything* was at a dead still.

The swells picked up the slack. In Oxford and Cambridge, the boys started manning trains and got the milk delivered for the babies in London. Eventually there was milk and food for everyone, and the old town ran quite well. We discovered that these charming old dowagers in black lace dresses we'd meet—in those days, people who were older looked older, dressed older, acted older, *were* older— were all working around the clock—as telephone operators at the *Evening Standard*, for instance—to keep things going.

But what I remember best about the General Strike was motoring down to Maidenhead one day. We went in an open Bentley, and I was sitting in front with the driver when a man jumped on the running board.

"Don't be frightened, madam," the man said. "It's quite all right. But may I please suggest that *perhaps* you *might* . . . you see, we're just turning a bus over down the road, and I thought you might be more comfortable if you made a *slight* detour."

I've never forgotten it. Oh, but I think that thoughtfulness and manners are everything.

I've know the English. I've known their hearts and their courage and their fascination and their conversation and their ways and their means—the whole bit. Did you know Lord Astor of Hever? Quite a good artist. You'll remember that Churchill said that all English gentlemen were taught how to read, write, and paint. Lord Astor was enchanting, absolutely divine. His children were friends of ours, but a wild lot. They used to stay out in London too late, and he'd say: "If you're not back at Hever at such-and-such a time, the draw-bridge is up. You don't get in!" So they'd stay in London a wee bit late, and when they'd arrive the drawbridge would be up. So there they were. Damn cold, as I don't have to tell you, in the middle of the night in the English countryside . . . no place to stay. What were they going to do? No way of getting the bridge down over the moat except from the castle's side. While a wet moat is considered most luxurious, it's nothing to be on the wrong side of at four in the morning. Fortunately, Lord Astor's passion in life was his dogs, so the children out there beyond the moat would start to bark, and that would get the *real* dogs barking. They'd all bark together, which would wake up the old boy, and he'd stump—he'd lost one leg in the First World War—through the castle, down through the great hall, through the corridors, past the great armory collection, the Holbeins, then an Elizabeth, then a Henry VIII, and then some of the wives he beheaded, and let down the bridge: "My darlings!" Here's this divine old gentleman in the middle of the night freezing to death in a nightshirt.

Then, of course, taxes made it impossible for him. He took it very quietly, left England, gave Hever to the eldest son, and moved to the south of France and painted his days away until he died. Then they had that great sale: finest armor in the world.

I have a passion for armor. To me, a gauntlet is the most beautiful thing. The golden fingers, the wrist line.

I always have armor in my Metropolitan shows. You don't notice them? In "Vanity Fair" I had a very beautiful lace room, and in the middle of it I had a gold breastplate. It was swollen gold . . . and out of the neck poured *point de Bruxelles,* the most beautiful lace in the world. The combination of gold and steel and lace!—no combination as beautiful.

Oh, I'm mad about armor. *Mad* about it! I love the way it's put together. I love the helmets with the feathers out the back. Milanese, you see. Have you ever seen a tilting green? It's the most beautiful thing I ever saw. Once I went down to Dartington Hall in Devonshire to see the tilting green, and I've never seen anything so beautiful in my life. I don't know how long a tilting green is, half a mile or so, but it's the most beautiful grass you'll ever see. There are great banks that rise up on either side like giant steps terraced in grass —grass, grass, green grass—where they set the silken tents dripping with tassels and gold . . . trouvères and troubadours strolling the grounds and beautiful women sitting out in front to watch. And all this wonderful green ground, with the knights in armor, banners, and these great horses. You can say, "Well, give me a good game of football." But that must have been the most beautiful contest to see in the world. You can't imagine it until you've seen a tilting green. All green, green, green, right to the sky.

CHAPTER SIXTEEN

Violet is a color I really like. But then I like almost every color. I have an eye for color—perhaps the most exceptional gift I have. Color depends entirely on the tonality. Green, for instance, can look like the subway—but if you get the *right* green . . . a spring green, for instance, is *marvelous*. The green of England and the green of France are the most beautiful spring greens. The green of England is a *little* deeper than the green of France, a *little* darker. . . .

Red is the great clarifier—bright, cleansing, and revealing. It makes all other colors beautiful. I can't imagine becoming bored with red—it would be like becoming bored with the person you love.

All my life I've pursued the perfect red. I can never get painters to mix it for me. It's exactly as if I'd said, "I want rococo with a spot of Gothic in it and a bit of Buddhist temple"—they have *no* idea what I'm talking about. About the best red is to copy the color of a child's cap in *any* Renaissance portrait.

I loathe red with *any* orange in it—although, curiously enough, I also loathe orange *without* red in it. When I say "orange," I don't mean yellow-orange, I mean *red*-orange—the orange of Bakst and Diaghilev, the orange that changed the *century*.

At the same time, I love nineteenth-century colors. I love the *names* of the colors of men's clothes of the Regency period—buff, sand, fawn . . . and don't forget snuff! My God, there were *words* in those days. But where is snuff today?

Balenciaga had the most wonderful sense of color—his *tête de nègre*, his *café au lait*, his violets, his magentas, and his mauves. Every summer I'd take his same four pairs of slacks and his same four pullovers to Southampton with me. Then . . . one year I went down to Biarritz. I laid out *exactly* the same four pairs of slacks, *exactly* the same four pullovers . . . and I'd never seen them before! It's the light, of course—the intensifying light of the Basque country. There's never been such a light. That was Balenciaga's country.

Lighting is everything in a color. It's affected by the way the sun shines in certain countries. And the farther north you go, the more sense of color you get. I'm not talking about little gray stone Scottish villages . . . but the *roses* of Scotland are so rose-pink! And the *purple heather*—the violent violet of heather under the blue Scottish sky . . . I adore Scotland. If only I didn't have to sleep there at night—it's so bloody cold.

I don't like southern skies. To me, they're not . . . enough. Although the most beautiful sky I've ever seen in my life was in the tropics, over Bahia—until I saw *exactly* the same sky over Hong Kong. I'd been told in Bahia that the only other place where that special blue existed was China, although they couldn't be farther apart. Bahia is practically on the equator, and most of China is very cold northern country; but the blue of the sky is *identical*. It's a *cold* blue of *hard* enamel, and it's *too* beautiful.

There's never been a blue like the blue of the Duke of Windsor's eyes. When I'd walk into the house in Neuilly, he'd be standing at the end of the hall. He always received you himself, which was terribly attractive, and he always had something funny and friendly to say to you while you disposed of your coat. But I'd see him standing there, and even in the light of the hall, which was quite dim, I could see that *blue*. It comes from being at sea. Sailors have it. I suppose it's in the family—Queen Mary had it too. But he had an aura of blue around him. I mean what I say—it was an azure aura surrounding the face. Even in a black-and-white picture you can feel it.

Black is the hardest color in the *world* to get *right*—except for gray.

Pauline de Rothschild, when she was Pauline Potter, lived in a house in New York where everyone used to argue about what color she'd had the drawing-room walls painted. I can tell you what it was. It was a light gunmetal gray—the color of the *inside* of a pearl.

In Paris, Molyneux had a salon painted and carpeted in another *perfect* shade of gray. All his *vendeuses* wore crêpe-de-chine dresses of the *exact* same color. Everything was gray so that the clothes he was showing would stand out. You saw *nothing* except the clothes he showed.

The Eskimos, I'm told, have seventeen different words for shades of *white*. This is even more than there are in *my* imagination.

But don't you *adore* the look of white silk slippers with the dark hem of a velvet dress? For months at *Harper's Bazaar* I went around saying, "Remember Velásquez!" That was one of my ideas that never reached the general public.

Purple is a beautiful color—a bit overdone at the moment because people have been so slow to take to it. It's associated with the church—ecclesiastical and powerful things—and it's also very Japanese, although it isn't really a purple the Japanese like. They prefer a sort of currant red with a *little* violet in it.

Taxicab yellow is *marvelous*. I often asked for taxicab-yellow backgrounds when I worked in photography studios.

At *Harper's Bazaar* a story went around about me: Apparently, I'd wanted a billiard-table green background for a picture. So the photographer went out and took the picture. I didn't like it. He went out and took it again. I didn't like it. Then . . . he went out and took it *again* and I *still* didn't like it. "I asked for billiard-table green!" I'm supposed to have said.

"But this *is* a billiard table, Mrs. Vreeland," the photographer replied.

"My dear," I apparently said, "I meant the *idea* of billiard-table green, not a *billiard table*."

This story is apocryphal, but it could well be true. The other day someone was talking about the idea of painting a room the color of the pupil of an eye in a Vermeer painting. I understand this *totally*.

Actually, pale-pink salmon is the *only* color I cannot *abide*—although, naturally, I adore pink. I love the pale Persian pinks of the little carnations of Provence and Schiaparelli's pink, the pink of the Incas. . . .

And though it's so *vieux jeu* I can hardly bear to repeat it—pink *is* the navy blue of India.

Oh, but violets. You should have seen Balenciaga's violets. He was the greatest dressmaker who ever lived. Those were the days when people dressed for dinner, and I mean *dressed*—not just changed their clothes. If a woman came in in a Balenciaga dress, no other woman in the room existed.

He wasn't interested in youth. He didn't care a bit about bones or anything to do with what we admire today. Oh, those collections! They were the most thrilling things! We'd stand in the corner of the salon if we couldn't get a chair to see his collections. You've never seen such colors—you've never seen such violets! My God, pink violets, blue violets! Suddenly you were in a nunnery, you were in a monastery.

Nobody else compared to him.

His voice was very low, and often you had to concentrate to hear it. His first name was Cristobal. His inspiration came from the bullrings, the flamenco dancers, the loose blouses the fishermen wear, the cool of the cloisters . . . and he took these moods and colors and, adapting them to his own tastes, literally dressed those who cared about such things for *thirty* years. He loved the coquetry of lace and ribbon, and yet he believed totally in the dignity of women. Balenciaga often said that women did not have to be perfect or beautiful to wear his clothes. When they wore his clothes, they became beautiful.

One never knew what one was going to see at a Balenciaga opening. One fainted. It was possible to blow up and die. I remember at one show in the early sixties—one put on for clients rather than for commercial buyers—Audrey Hepburn turned to me and asked why I wasn't frothing at the mouth at what I was seeing. I told her I was trying to act calm and detached because, after all, I was a member of the press. Across the way Gloria Guinness was sliding out of her chair onto the floor. Everyone was going up in foam and thunder. We didn't know what we were *doing*, it was so glorious. Well, what was going on was that Balenciaga was introducing the maillot for the first time. A maillot is like a body stocking, closed at the neck, ankle, and wrist. At this show it was a nude color, half-gold and pink, and over it was a tent of chiffon surrounding the model, the girl. It was *incredibly* beautiful. And don't forget, Balenciaga didn't use long-legged models—he used rather short-limbed, plump models, because he liked Spanish women. It was the most exciting garment I've ever seen. It was a dream. And do you know, I tried to get it for my Balenciaga show at the Met and no one could even remember it—how like a dream it had passed!

And then one day Balenciaga just closed his doors. He never even told Bunny Mellon, who of course was his greatest client . . . I suppose she had the greatest collection of Balenciagas in the world.

I was staying with Mona Bismark in Capri when the news came. I was downstairs, dressed for dinner, having a drink. Consuelo Crespi telephoned me from Rome, saying it had just come over the radio that Balenciaga had closed his doors forever that afternoon, and that he'd never open them again. Mona didn't come out of her room for three days. I mean, she went into a complete . . . I mean, it was the end of a certain part of her *life*!

CHAPTER SEVENTEEN

When people ask me what the greatest change in my life is, I always say it is Fear—the sense of imminent physical danger that we must all live with in big cities everywhere today.

I was once afraid of nothing. All those years on Seventh Avenue—the garment district—how many years was it? The years I was on *Vogue* I wasn't *that* much on Seventh Avenue, but on *Harper's Bazaar* I was the fashion editor. So I went there to see what they they had to offer. I tramped the streets. I covered the waterfront.

I'd walk home those sixty blocks alone all those years. I *loved* the fur district, and that's where I'd walk when I finished working.

These are the war years I'm speaking about now. Believe me, there were no cabs; I'd walk these *long, long* blocks. We were practically in a blackout—what they called a brownout—the lights were very dim. I was absolutely *freezing*. There weren't slacks in those days, and there weren't boots—I was in sandals. I had a fur coat on—a fur-lined raincoat—and I'd just *shout* to myself, "Keep walking! Keep walking!"

I did this evening after evening. I took it as much for granted as the fact that I'm going to sleep in my own bed tonight.

When I got home, I was alone. The boys were in the armed forces. Reed was living in Montreal through the whole war, working for British interests. He was there for seven years. We were married for forty-six years, and for seven of them he was away. It was a very vivid period in my life. For seven years, I was by myself. . . .

But I was so happy when I was down on Seventh Avenue. I was always going up rusty staircases with old newspapers lying all over the place and the most ghastly-looking characters hanging around . . . but *nothing* was frightening to me. It was *all* part of the great adventure, my métier, the scene. I suppose that's why I have such a devotion to Seventh Avenue today—because the whole bit was interesting to me. So many of them were Jewish refugees. Hardly spoke English. They meant a great deal to me because they provided a touch of old Europe. It wasn't a letdown, even after Chanel. After all, it was my world. The men down there were my pals. They were the people who looked after me. They were the people who made my life *possible*.

I never wore clothes from Seventh Avenue myself, you understand. I always kept a totally European view of things. Maybe that's why I was so appreciated there. I was independent. In those days, don't forget, fashion traveled very slowly. When I arrived back in this country after the war started, I couldn't believe what I saw. In the summer, every woman wore diamond clips on crêpe de chine dresses. And they all wore silk stockings—this was before nylons—under these hideous strappy high heels. This is in the summer, you understand—in the *country*. It was *unbelievable*.

For years in Europe I'd been bare-legged and thong-sandaled once the heat came on. I still have some of my original sandals I had made in Capri in 1935 when Reed and I were staying at the Fortino on the Marina Grande. The theory of the sandals was that the sandal strap went between the toes. The soles of these sandals were so beautiful. They were built up in layers thinner than my fingernail—layer upon layer. When you walked, it was like walking in satin. In Capri, we used to walk up through the hills, through the vineyards, and all the way out to Tiberius's palace—that's a hell of a walk. I can remember Coco Chanel and Visconti used to do it on donkeys. She'd wear her beret and her pullover and her white duck pants—and her pearls, naturally—and the donkey would carry her uphill over this steep, rocky road. Visconti was infatuated with her, and he'd follow her on his donkey. Capri—pagan and wonderful.

Then the war came, and there was no more communication among any of us. But I had the sandals. And I gave them to a shoemaker from New Jersey called Mr. Maxwell and asked him to copy them. He'd never seen anything like them. So I told him the story of where *I'd* copied them from—the pornographic museum at Pompeii, which had originally been open only to men. Those were the days of boat trips on the Mediterranean, and these old maids would save up their money for years, get themselves men's suits, and get into the museum, where they'd holler and yell and scream and be found epileptic on the floor. It was *unbelievable*. The police would be brought in, these old maids would be carried out on stretchers, and eventually the museum had to be closed down entirely.

Through a friend in the Mussolini government, I was able to get in. "Nothing could be easier to arrange," he said.

So I *saw*. . . . In Pompeii, everything that can happen in life was captured in the minute and a half a volcanic eruption takes. Women are having babies, dogs scratching their backs . . . *held* forever in eternity. And in the museum I saw a woman having an affair with her slave, who was wearing . . .

I was telling all this to Mr. Maxwell, who, naturally, was absolutely horrified. He was the most charming, gentle soul—reeked of all the nicest Englewood, New Jersey, characteristics—but he'd never heard a *woman* discuss such things. But I went on. . . .

The slave was wearing link slave bracelets, which I recognized immediately, because everyone had worn slave bracelets exactly like them in the twenties. But then . . . instead of the very elaborate sandals of a *grand seigneur* or a warrior, or the sandals of a gentleman of the town or a tradesman, he wore the simplest sandal in the world. It had just *one* thong which went between the big toe and the one next to it, and *one* strap around the ankle attached to the heel.

You ask why he was making love wearing his sandals? He probably wasn't given the *time*. She probably jumped him and he didn't have a chance to get those sandals off; and then, of course, Vesuvius knocked them both to the floor. This was the design I took to Capri, where they made the sandals up for me from my description.

Eventually, Mr. Maxwell got over his shock. He copied the sandals. But no one could wear them. Apparently, there was something in the health regulations of New York City that said that no one could try on shoes unless she was wearing stockings. Obviously, the thong couldn't go over a stocking and between the toes, and of course that was the *whole point*. Somehow or other, the law was changed. Don't ask me how—I've never concerned myself with that sort of thing. But from then on there was a very nice business for Mr. Maxwell.

That was the Birth of the Thonged Sandal. The fingernails came next.

When I arrived in America, I had these very dark red nails which some people objected to, but then some people object to absolutely everything. The point is that they were absolutely clear and perfect. There was only one other woman in New York with perfect nails, and that was Mona Williams, who had a manicurist come to her every evening. In those days, you had your fingernails done at home for a very good reason—the varnish took *forever* to dry, and you couldn't use your hands for hours and hours. I had mine done at home, but they dried almost instantly, and that's what this story is about.

In Paris I'd had a manicurist, a Venetian named Perrera, who'd been in the chicken-farm business with Catherine d'Erlanger—the one who lived in Lord Byron's house at the end of Piccadilly. She also had a house outside of Venice, up the Brenta where there're those strange canals and those wonderful sixteenth-century houses. Her house, Villa Malcontenta, had Veronese walls and ceilings. Perrera was, I suppose, what you'd call a "peasant"—though I hate to use words which I don't quite know the meaning of; I merely mean that he wasn't a man of the aristocracy. He was in all kinds of businesses, but what he loved more than anything else in the world was women's hands. When he came in the evening to my room in Paris, I don't think he would have noticed if I'd been naked. I'm not sure he ever looked at my face.

Certain men adore women for certain things and that becomes their life. Perrera's life was being with women with beautiful hands. He *worshiped* Barbara Hutton, for instance, who had the most beautiful hands in the world. He talked about them endlessly. Perrera was far from being a rich man. I'm sure that when he left Barbara Hutton, he'd walk through the rain of Paris to the nearest Métro and come home to a very simple life. His price, you see, was almost nothing—he took care of women's hands just for *love*.

He'd come in . . . and he'd undo this beautiful gray suede fitted case and take out his instruments, which were all gold—they'd been given to him by Ena, the Queen of Spain, granddaughter of Victoria. He had this *wonderful* varnish—don't ask me where *he* made it—that dried *as* he painted it on. You could have nails out to *here*, which I used to have, and they'd dry instantly.

Do you want to know what the artist Bébé Bérard liked more than anything else in the world? He liked to watch Perrera paint fingernails with this varnish—the *artistry* of it. Bérard saw this being done to me once in my hotel room and couldn't wait for the next time.

I can remember the last time I saw Perrera right after war was declared. We said goodbye and *au revoir* and "It won't be long" and "It isn't really a war" . . . and I brought two big flacons of his varnish with me to New York. I gave them to my little manicurist, who was sort of a free swinger in that she didn't work for a manicure parlor, but went from door to door. And one day the varnish ran out. Naturally, I was in a state.

"I've got a boyfriend downtown," my little manicurist said, "and I think I can get him to copy it."

"Oh," I said, "who is he?"

"Well, he makes a nail varnish that everyone's crazy about."

His name was Revson. He was working on about Twenty-seventh Street and Sixth Avenue in a place with an old iron staircase up the back. His varnish had a great color, and it didn't chip—which was the biggest thing—but it took hours to dry, and it had no staying power.

But then—from studying Perrera's—he evolved a product that dried faster than anything anyone had ever used in America. And after a few years, he started to get pretty big. In fact, he became the biggest—the *most*.

Today, the great varnish of the world that covers the *waterfront* is Revlon. And, curiously enough, whenever I saw him there was always something in Charles Revson's eye . . . I always knew that *he* knew that *I* knew that he had made this incredible fortune off of one small bottle of mine with maybe *this* much left in it. Yes, there was always something in his eye. . . .

The first thing I did after the war was to try to find Perrera. No one—but *no* one—ever found him, not in Venice, not in Paris, not in the south of France. He disappeared off the face of the earth. I'd wanted to bring him to America to put him together with . . . well, I had the business connections. But I have always been very naïve when it comes to business.

Reed and I *never* discussed business. It would have bored him to *death*. I never said to him, "Don't you think I should go to this man Revson and say, 'Look, I can do with a quarter of a half of a tenth of a percent of what you're making today because it was my varnish that made your life as it is today possible'?"

"So what?" Reed would have said. "You got the varnish you needed—what else do you want?"

CHAPTER

EIGHTEEN

I remember the night Reed and I arrived in Paris right after the war. Oh, how it had changed! Potato flour. To think that one was eating French bread, the great French triumph, made of potatoes! Everyone was in wooden shoes. *Clack clack clack.* You could tell the time of day from your hotel room by the sound of wooden soles on the pavement. If there was a great storm of them, it meant that it was lunch hour and people were leaving their offices for the restaurants. Then there'd be another great clatter when they returned to the office, et cetera et cetera. . . . The day we arrived it just happened to be Bastille Day, although we hadn't planned it that way. The fountains on the place de la Concorde were playing for the first time since the liberation. And we drove all over Paris. We went everywhere—Chaillot, St. Denis . . . I forget the names of the *quartiers* above Montmartre, but we went to all of them. Every little square had the most ghastly little band playing the same ghastly little tune.

Strangers were dancing with strangers. Girls were dancing with girls. Strange young men who looked haunted—as if they hadn't been out of a cellar in years—were dancing with fat old women. It was raining. No one was speaking. It was hideous—and marvelous.

At what must have been four o'clock in the morning, I

suddenly realized I was hungry. So we picked this little street above Montmartre, and on it was a restaurant that looked awfully nice, but the shutters were closed. So we banged and banged on the shutters until a man came out.

"We've had nothing to eat," I said. "We've just arrived from America and we've been spending this wonderful night in Paris, but we're so *hungry*."

"*Mais entrez, madame et monsieur!*" the man said. "*Entrez! C'est une auberge!*"

I've never forgotten that, because, for me, France has always been an *auberge*—for feelings, for emotion, and for so many other things. Reed and I spoke of that experience for years after. The man opened up the door so wide that he could not have made a greater gesture if it had been the Hall of Mirrors!

Paris! I was so excited. But Paris had changed. The world had changed.

I realized this when I went for my fittings. You don't know what a part of life fittings once were. Remember I told you that before the war I used to have three fittings on a *nightgown*—and I'm not *that* deformed.

After the war you were no longer fitted for nightgowns.

Other things had changed. Couture before the war wasn't that expensive. It was hard to pay more than two hundred dollars for a dress. I had been what was known as a *mannequin du monde*—meaning "of the world"—because I was out every night in every nightclub, seen, seen, seen. . . . I was always given by the *maison de couture* for being a *mannequin du monde* what was known as a *prix jeune fille*—that is to say, they would give me the dress to wear and keep. The phrase no longer exists in the French vocabulary. The first thing I asked after the war was: "Does it still exist—as an expression?" I wasn't hinting around.

"Absolutely not!" I was told. "It's as dead as mud."

Before the war everybody in London and Paris was dressed by somebody. I remember Reed always used to say about plump old Elsa Maxwell, for instance, who never had a cent: "The great thing

about Elsa is that she's dressed by Patou." She'd slip off these jackets
—this *enormous* mountain of a women—and there would be the label
"Jean Patou."

Elsa wasn't a vulgar woman. This is hard to explain to
someone who never knew her, because she *looked* vulgar. You see
pictures of her where she looks like a cook on her night out. The end
of her nose was vulgar. Why wasn't she? I don't know.

Maybe it was because she adored music so much. She was a
sublime pianist. A love of music is a great purifier, and music was as
clear as crystal water to her.

Do you remember Mary Borden's *A Woman with White
Eyes?* In that book is a marvelous description of fat white hands
galloping over the keys. They were Elsa's. She started as an entertainer. Then, of course, she became famous for her parties. She'd
whip it up in your own home. She'd take it over. These days everyone
goes out to restaurants, but in her day Elsa would give the party in
your home, invite all the important people, and you'd get a bill for
the food, flowers, and wine. She herself never had a glass of port.
She was not nobody. She always dined with kings. Nice kings. The
King of Sweden. She watched him play tennis. She'd stay in any
hotel that would pick up the tab. She started up roaring things around
her in the Waldorf and ended up in the Summit. The chandelier in
Elsa's apartment in the Summit wasn't exactly in the center of the
room; it made you feel kind of wonky.

I remember a dinner with her in Paris before the war. I
was seated opposite a San Franciscan named Tony Montgomery, who
was one of the playboys of the period, and we heard some Frenchman
saying to Elsa, "And, Miss Maxwell, were you in San Francisco during the great earthquake?"—you know, conversation at dinner.

"Of course I was there," she said, "and I can remember
it very well. I was walking down the marble staircase in my father's
house when, suddenly, the staircase cracked under my feet. . . ."

Tony gave me a look and I gave him a look. We both knew
that there weren't *any* marble staircases west of the Mississippi in
those days—let alone in Elsa's father's house. But that was Elsa—she

was just putting on the ritz, keeping things up. Why say you were born in a hovel? Who wants to hear that?

She always kept the ball in the air. But I can remember one time when I saw her totally tongue-tied. She had called me.

"Diana, do you want to meet Christine Jorgensen?"

"Actually," I said, "I haven't thought of it."

"Well, I thought it might interest you. You're in all sorts of businesses, and who knows? It might be a revelation to you. I'm giving a lunch tomorrow. . . ."

Naturally, I went. What year was this? It was after the war. Look it up—it was whatever year it was when Christine Jorgensen was the focus of the world, publicly recognized for, shall we say, three weeks, for being the first known transsexual. The lunch was in Elsa's private room upstairs in a hotel salon. Leland Hayward was there, Fulco di Verdura, the great jewelry designer, and several other very fascinating men I can't remember. And no one could think of a single word to say to this very well-mannered, very charming person called Christine Jorgensen. We stared at her and had no idea how to begin. What *would* one ask: "What's the first thing you did—blow up your bazooms?" Fulco had never been so tongue-tied in his life. He wanted to ask about what she did about her underarms. Never did. Christine Jorgensen did the best *she* could to keep the ball in the air, talking about the food and the weather and, mmm . . . my *God*, the changes in this world! Elsa was *bouleversée*. It was the *only* time I ever saw her like that, and I knew her very well.

That first summer Reed and I spent in Europe after the war, Elsa invited us to an extraordinary evening in the south of France. We motored through Provence to Antibes. Ah, the light of Provence! We were having a sort of love affair with France, seeing again all the beauty we'd loved so much all our lives, smelling all the wonderful smells . . . little bluebells, little Persian pinks, and all the other delicious smells of Provence. We spent the nights in such luxury on real linen sheets in the most divine *auberges* after wonderful dinners and walks after dinner under the pines. . . .

Then we arrived in Antibes. Everyone was waterskiing.

Every girl was in a bikini. At the time, I said that the bikini was the biggest thing since the atom bomb, but I suppose bikinis started *during* the war—they probably just tore bedsheets apart and made them. It was the year of "La Vie en rose." We'd go to bed rather early every night at the Hôtel du Cap, and we'd hear people walking home—everyone singing "La Vie en rose." Songs last forever. They fix particular years in your mind. That year, everyone was singing that song to everyone else into the night, and we'd lie there and listen to the happiness . . . it was all "La Vie en rose." The air is so still there. It holds music. Do you know what I mean?

Reed, naturally, was dressed and ready to go long before I was in the morning. He was wonderful to travel with because he'd always get up early, case the joint, then come back and pick me up, and together we'd share what he'd found to see or do. And one morning he ran into this Argentinian, Dodero. Dodero was one of Perón's henchmen—well born, well educated, very charming, and his manners were magnificent. He invited us to come to his villa in Cannes for a party the next night. Reed told him that we had already agreed to dine with Elsa Maxwell that evening but that we'd try to come by after dinner.

Elsa's dinner was for Maurice Chevalier. It was in the old port of Antibes, which very few people have bothered to see. Elsa had taken over the main street, which led down to the docks, and set up one long table. I was right across the table from Chevalier. Of course, I'd been looking at him since I was sixteen years old, coming down the steps of the stage of the Casino de Paris, but now I actually *saw* him. My *God*, what an attractive man, and what a fascinator! It must be wonderful to feel that the world loves you and that you have something to give the world. I would think it's the best life going. Do I love a boulevardier! The way he wore a hat! Carried a stick!

After dinner, we went up in the hills above Cannes to the Dodero party, past several of his henchmen—when henchmen have henchmen, you know they're *big*—and through an absolutely empty villa. Obviously, no one slept there or lived there—heaven knows what they used it for. Then there were steps down through the pine groves, and this charming man, Dodero, came up the steps, took hold of my hand, and kissed it. I felt this terrific beat in his hands and realized he was a very sick man—the tension of the life he was leading as part of the Perón setup was too much for him. It was obvious he lived in terrible danger all the time. That summer he had three floors of the Hotel Carlton, three yachts in the harbor, and then three villas in the hills behind Cannes. It was the *most* mysterious setup.

But we walked with him down this long flight of steps into a beautiful place that had been cut away as a dance floor, and he showed us to our table. Soon there were little gold chairs pulled up all around it. People began to arrive. All the old playboys from before the war—I can't remember any of their names—stopped by the table. All of the girls came up to me because they were our models from New York. Everyone was terribly attractive.

I've always been so flattered that anyone, whatever his status, feels he can ask me to a party. Reed and I could dine with a king one night and the next night go to a party like this one . . . which was the last, I would say, of the demimonde. The demimonde—the mystery of those women! Men have always been able to take any background they wished for themselves. I was being read Proust the other evening, and a demimondaine turns up at a party—no raised eyebrows—at a party for the Duchesse de Guermantes. They're still around, I'm sure, but no one gives parties for them anymore. No one even uses the expression anymore but me. It's antique as a word, like *risqué*, like *roué*, like *outré* . . . they're all terribly out of date.

The demimondaines were not the only ones there that night. In every sense it was a perfectly respectable party. I came in a sleeveless short dress. Summer clothes. It was a magically memorable evening. The waiters were wonderful. The lights were draped through the groves. It was the night Rita Hayworth, who was certainly the best-looking thing we ever had in America, met Aly Khan—we saw the meeting. It was the night Tyrone Power met Linda Christian—we saw the meeting. And this was the night I met a girl named Carroll McDaniel. She later married Fon, the Marquis de Portago, whose special passion was racing cars. You'll remember that Fon stopped in the middle of a car race, the Mille Miglia, for some oil, and across the track came Linda Christian, who by then had given up Tyrone Power. She leaned into the racecar and kissed him. The Kiss of Death: He was dead seven minutes later in a crash.

His mother was one of those great Irish girls who get more freckles if they cross a street. She broke her leg skiing when she must have been eighty, had it set in a cast, and started skiing again. She once told me a wonderful story about herself. It was during the war, and we were sitting on the Southampton beach. On the *beach*—she was wearing bracelets with green pears like *this* falling from marquise diamonds like *that*—it took just a few stones to go around the wrists. She told me she had once been a nurse in the Government Hospital in Dublin. The elderly person she was looking after asked her if he could take her home to be his private nurse because he was dying and couldn't be without one. She had nothing else on her plate, and he was a very nice old man. They got married.

At some point he realized that there was no reason for going on, and he took her hand and said, "Tell me—if I were not so rich, would you have been so kind to me?"

"No," she said.

"Would you have married me?"

"No."

So he said, "You're the most honest girl in the whole world. For that, you will inherit everything."

So the richest widow in Europe hit Spain, married the most eligible man in Europe, the Marquis de Portago—the King of Spain's godson—gave birth to Fon, the King of Spain's namesake, who later married, as I've already told you . . . look here, you musn't let me *repeat* myself!

CHAPTER
NINETEEN

In my leisure time I appear rather . . . impractical. But I do think that I've made a practical woman out of myself. You can't have worked the number of years I have, through hell and high water, without being *basically* practical.

A man has a disciplined, clear mind and a sense of language. When he writes a business letter, for instance, it's with total authority—there can't be a comma wrong or a semicolon wrong or a word with two sides to it. Whereas a woman . . . I had to learn discipline. And it was men—particularly Reed Vreeland—who taught it to me.

By the time I moved back to America and went to work, I was quite well formed in the discipline department. Very few women had affected me. Carmel Snow, the editor of *Harper's Bazaar*, certainly had no effect on me when I arrived. In fact, in a curious way, I think she resented my taste. But I know I was always influenced by Elsie Mendl.

Elsie had total discipline. You could see her discipline in the way she'd arrange flowers, in the way she'd plan a meal . . . in the way she did everything. Everything had a plan. She was very American in that way, but she also had a great understanding of the French eighteenth century, which was a very logical time for women.

I adored her house at Versailles and the way everything smelled of lavender and the way her windows would be half-open when it was raining outside and the way she'd arranged her zoo of topiary animals just outside the windows, which was *too* charming . . . but it was all done with authority. She called a spade a *spade*.

Elsie, naturally, had wonderful taste, like everyone I knew in Europe. Of course, one is born with good taste. It's very hard to acquire. You can acquire the *patina* of taste. But what Elsie Mendl had was something else that's particularly American—an appreciation of vulgarity. Vulgarity is a very important ingredient in life. I'm a great believer in vulgarity—if it's got vitality. A little bad taste is like a nice splash of paprika. We all need a splash of bad taste—it's hearty, it's healthy, it's physical. I think we could use *more* of it. *No* taste is what I'm against.

What catches my eye in a window is the hideous stuff— the *junk*. Plastic *ducks*! This was why Reed would never go walking in any city with me. "If you'd occasionally stop in front of a window where there might be *something* . . ." he said. "But as you go straight to the ugliest things, I won't walk with you unless we go straight to the park."

Do you know anyone why buys plaster poodles? A few years ago Jerry Zipkin met me in Palm Beach. Now Jerry Zipkin's a good friend because he's constructive. He's destructive *and* constructive, and you know what *that* means. That means he pulls you apart— but then he puts you back together again *better*. I'll give you an example. I probably hadn't been in Palm Beach in thirty years. When I arrived Jerry said, "May I have the honor of taking you down Worth Avenue?" Well, I had a vista ahead that I could not have imagined! We saw plaster poodles, painted pink—quite a beautiful pink, actually, like a Du Barry rose—and we saw picture frames with plaster angels, painted pink, of course, and mirrors and shells. On the right side, the left side, the poodles, the angels. Everything was either plaster or jewelry—not jewels but jewelry. Apparently, they can't keep the poodles in stock—not possibly. It was the *goddamnedest* thing. End-less. Forever. Who buys them? I was alarmed. "Jerry," I said, "let's stop this. I think I've got the *hang* of it. Don't you think we've *had* Worth Avenue?"

"You haven't seen anything yet," he said. "I'm going to take you to a place where I *doubt* you'll get in."

So we went to a place on Mizner Court, I thinks it's called, and Jerry said, "Let me explain it to you—you have to be a member."

"But Jerry," I said, "I thought you were taking me to a shop."

"It *is* a shop," he said. "But the *chances* are—don't be offended—that you won't get in. We'll just have to see what we can arrange. . . ."

Then . . . we took an abrupt turn to the right, into a court; we rang the bell and a man came out. "Oh, Madame Vreeland," he said—it couldn't be more American, the "Madame Vreeland." . . . He gave me a big kiss. He turned out to be a leftover from my Seventh Avenue days. He presented me with a year's free member-ship. Very nice of him. Apparently for fifty dollars a year you could shop there! I couldn't believe it—you had to *pay* to *buy*.

The shop had an Oriental, rather exotic atmosphere about it—beautiful tisanes, imports from China, picture frames, lengths of Oriental cloth. I don't know why it was so private. Perhaps they didn't want the plaster poodle trade in there.

CHAPTER

TWENTY

There's no such thing as a slack French face. Haven't you ever noticed that? I've given this a lot of thought, and I think it's because the French have to exercise their jaws and the inside of their mouths so much just to get the words *out*. The vowels demand so much. In fact, the French language has a lot to do with the handsomeness and the beauty of the French face. Talk one line in French and the whole inside of your face moves, whereas the English language leaves you a bit slack. I'll give you an example: Look in the mirror. Now say *"Ché-rie!"* Did you see what your face just did? Did you see all the exercise you got? Now try "Dear." No exercise there. You're really on a dead horse. Don't you love that phrase? A friend of mine and I once got out of a movie house across from Bloomingdale's and we stepped into a taxi standing there at curbside. A guy leaned in the back window and said, "Hey, you're on a dead horse. No driver." We looked, and sure enough there wasn't anybody in the front seat. Heaven knows where he was. In the movie house? Perhaps he was off having a hamburger.

But to get on with it, there never was a more French face than de Gaulle's. France was . . . de Gaulle. And, as you know, the French like the French very much. De Gaulle was full of the old *amour propre,* all right—he *loved* himself. And he was my hero, as he was for much of France and much of the world for many, many years.

In the middle sixties he'd fallen out of favor. I'd just arrived in Paris to cover the collections, and I was dining with the young married set—all very charming but rather *comme il faut,* shall we say. I was full of my own worth. So I said, "You know, when anything extraordinary happens here, you can't take it. Now take de Gaulle—"

"Oh!" They went to pieces. "You're not going to try and sell us *de Gaulle?*"

"I'm not selling," I said, "I'm only telling you."

"But we're thinking of our *country!*"

"I am, too. I don't live here, but I know heroes. You've got to have a hero. You've got to have a face. You've got to have a leading man. I'll give you an example: If *everyone* at this table was responsible for ordering the dinner, would we ever get a bite to eat?"

Then I went on: "How many people will come through the corridors—through the *bloodstream*—of history in the last fifty years the way de Gaulle will? Who fought so that France would continue to exist? When there was no place for him to fight here, who went to London and waited like an errand boy for Churchill to listen to him? Why, I don't understand why you're treating him the way you are. Do you think that whatever is bourgeois and ordinary and 'so what?' is great? Anything *extra*ordinary . . . that's really what France stands for—the supreme logic of the extraordinary!"

I really gave them a bit of what for!

The next day I got a call from one of the chaps at the table.

"Diana, we believe in desire and passion. When anyone loves with your passion, they should be closer to the person they love, so I've arranged for you to go to his press conference. I will hold your seat for you. Come as soon as you can."

As soon as I'd hung up the phone, I turned to Reed and told him what had happened. I said to Reed, "Chanel is opening this afternoon at three-thirty—I can't possibly do it!"

"Why?" he said.

"Well," I said, "because Chanel is . . . I mean, after all, I'm *paid* to cover these collections."

I had the most marvelous husband. He was always on the right side. He always knew what to do and what to say to me.

"You *are*? What's the matter with you? You're so cracked about this fellow de Gaulle, and you get this unique opportunity, everything arranged for you, and you bring up *Chanel*, whose clothes you've only been looking at since 1925!"

So I sent a message to Mademoiselle Chanel saying that, unfortunately, I'd broken a tooth on a piece of bread (which was a very good excuse—all Americans *do* on French crusts) and that I couldn't attend.

Well, I went to the press conference. I arrived at the Elysée Palace, but I didn't have my passport. "*Passeport, madame, passeport!*" the gendarmes said. It was rather windy, so their capes sort of blew this way and I sort of went that way and went right on in. How could they keep me out?

I took my seat in the second row. And then, in the most beautiful voice—trained, I have no doubt, by the Comédie Française —my hero said, "*Mesdames, messieurs. . . .*"

I mean, the *beauty* of the language! The *pleading* for the morals! He had the most beautiful diction. And he had the hands of the Comédie Française, too—the hands of a leader, the hands, almost, of a messiah. It was the most thrilling experience.

I also made a great discovery. In the usual photograph you see of de Gaulle from the sixties he's almost totally bald. When I saw him I realized that his hairline was much closer to his face—a very distinguished hairline framing a small, completely refined, totally French face. Now, obviously, he wasn't done up for the photographs —this is the general of an army and the President of France! There was no monkey business *there*.

When I got back to the Crillon, where we were staying, after these splendid hours of being a part of this glorious man, my hero, there were red roses waiting for me—red red roses. They were from

Coco Chanel—the kind Chanel always sent, the kind that open, not the kind that shrivel up into a little walnut and die—and amongst them was the most charming note in Mademoiselle's own hand: *"Chère Diane, My plane waits for you at Le Bourget. It will take you to Lausanne, where you will see my dentist, the greatest in the world."*

Of course, I immediately had to send my own flowers and a note saying what a charming thought it had been on her part and that in the tooth department it hadn't been as bad as I had originally thought, et cetera, et cetera, and I would be able to come and see her show the next afternoon.

The next day she'd forgotten all about the tooth. I didn't have to explain *anything*. Which was fortunate. Chanel could not abide de Gaulle and shouted it from every rooftop.

Coco Chanel always fitted me in her private atelier six flights up in the house on the rue Cambon. First, there was the beautiful rolling staircase up to the salon floor—the famous mirrored staircase—and after that, you were practically on a *stepladder* for five more flights. It used to *kill* me. As soon as I'd arrive at the front door of the house, there'd be someone waiting, saying, *"Mademoiselle vous attend, madame."*

My God, I used to get up there so breathless! And then I'd get fitted. Coco was a nut on armholes. She never, ever got a armhole quite, *quite* perfect, the way she wanted it. She was always snipping and taking out sleeves, driving the tailors absolutely crazy. She'd put pins in me so I'd be contorted, and she'd be talking and talking and giving me all sorts of philosophical observations, such as "Live with rigor and vigor" or "Grow old like a man," and I'd say, "I think most men grow old like women, myself," and she'd say, "No, you're wrong, they've got logic, they've got a reality to them"—with my arm up in the air the whole time! Then if she *really* wanted to talk, she'd put pins in under both arms so I simply couldn't move, much less get a word in!

She watched the collections from the top of the mirrored stairs. She used to crouch there all alone, and when you went up to see her afterward, she knew *exactly* what you thought.

She was extraordinary. The *alertness* of the woman! The

charm! You would have fallen in love with her. She was mesmerizing, strange, alarming, witty . . . you can't compare anyone with Chanel. They haven't got the *chien*! Or the chic. She was French, don't forget —totally French!

Where she came from in France is anyone's guess. She said one thing one day and another thing the next. She was a peasant— and a genius. Peasants and geniuses are the only people who count, and she was both.

The Duke of Westminster and Grand Duke Dmitri were the two men in her life. Between them she learned everything there is to know about luxury, and no one's ever had a greater sense of luxury than Coco Chanel.

The Grand Duke Dmitri was *the* handsomest . . . the hang of his suits! His leg in a *boot*! Oh *God*! He was more interested in fishing and shooting—like all Russian men—but he was a beauty! Now, whether he killed Rasputin or not, who knows? He never lived out of his father's palace until he came to Paris, and then I don't think he had a bed to himself, he was so poor. Chanel discovered him and reinstated him; she got him beautiful rooms and wonderful valets and marvelous flannels and all the things that a gentleman likes. And from him she learned all about great jewels and great living. Then she went off with the Duke of Westminster. He was desperately in love with her, but she refused to marry him. She pointed out that there had already been three Duchesses of Westminster, but there would always be just one Coco Chanel. She learned about afternoon teas from him and about magnificently maintained country houses. She rode with him and became a splendid horsewoman. The Duke had about seven properties in England, the greatest property owner in the world save the Russians in the days of the Czars. Such elegance! Every inch a Duke! He had his shoelaces ironed every day. Insisted on it. But then that's nothing. Shoelaces were nothing to iron.

He was named after a horse—Bendor, who won the Derby. Lots of people were named after horses. One of my great friends in London was Lady Morvyth Menson. I asked, "For goodness' sakes, where'd you get this name Morvyth?" She said, "Well, you see, my father was off racing somewhere when I was born. My mother was dying, and there was no one in charge but the servants. 'We've got to name this child *something*.'" So they called her Morvyth after one of the polo ponies. Terribly pretty Welsh name, isn't it?

Well, most people get most things from something—I don't say *everything*, but most things. From the English, and from her life with the Duke of Westminster, Chanel learned luxury, and she copied the clean turnout of Eton boys and the men at shoots. And from Russia she copied the Romanov pearls. Dmitri got out of Russia the way you'd get out of a fire—but he had the pearls. He gave them to her, and she made copies of them which the women of the world have known and worn ever since, whether artificial or cultured—that long, long string. . . .

And the Russian clothes! I remember now that Coco used to go to Moscow quite regularly in the thirties. When I was there a few years ago with Tom Hoving, arranging the show of Russian costumes for the Metropolitan, I went to the Historical Museum, where I saw all the rich peasant dresses. When I got back to the hotel, Tom asked me what I'd seen. "Well," I said, "I saw a lot of marvelous clothes—most of which I've worn myself." He looked at me as if I were demented. "Actually," I said, "*literally*. . . . These were Chanel's clothes of the thirties—the big skirts, the small jackets, the headdresses. . . ."

A woman dressed by Chanel back in the twenties and the thirties—like a woman dressed by Balenciaga in the fifties and sixties—walked into a room and had a dignity, an authority, a thing beyond a question of taste.

I'm not speaking of the late Chanel, who amused herself by dressing the streets of Paris. When she reopened after the war, she wanted to see her suits all over the place. They say she showed the clothes to the copyists before she showed them to the customers or the press. She had reached the point in life where she'd done everything—*everything*—and she had to amuse herself.

These postwar suits of Chanel were designed God knows *when*, but the tailoring, the line, the shoulders, the underarms, the *jupe*—never too short, never making a fool of a woman when she sits down—is even today the right thing to wear.

When I first became friends with her in the middle thirties, Coco was extraordinarily good-looking. She was a bright, dark gold color—wide faced, with a snorting nose, just like a little bull, and deep Dubonnet-red cheeks. Before the war she lived in a house on the Faubourg St. Honoré. It had an enormous garden with fountains, the most beautiful salons opening on the garden, and something like fifty-four Coromandel screens shaping these rooms into the most extraordinary *allées* of charm. There she received the *world*. It was a proper society she had around her—artists, musicians, poets—and everyone was fascinated by her. Cocteau adored her, Bébe Bérard adored her, Picasso . . . who in those days drove around Paris with his latest mistress by his side in a bright yellow Hispano-Suiza with a hammer and sickle painted on the side. Definitely part of the scene!

Coco Chanel became a figure in all of this—Paris society—entirely through wit and taste. Her taste was what you'd call *formidable*. She was irresistible. Absolutely. About a year before she died, I got an invitation to dine with her at her apartment on the rue Cambon. It was for the Duke and Duchess of Windsor. Niki de Gunzburg had called me up and said, "Did you get this invitation from Coco? Well, then, I'll take you, because we're only going to be six, and we'll have a wonderful time."

I'd been so often in that marvelous drawing room of hers, that splendid dining room. The fire was burning. Wonderful bronze animals on the floor.

I had never seen those rooms the way they were that night. Everything was in a glow. The fire was discreet because it wasn't that cold, but it was Paris and therefore damp. Niki and I were the first to arrive. Then the Windsors were announced. Coco went forward, and I had never seen a woman look at a man the way she welcomed him. I can't put it into words. Their drinks were brought to them. They never looked away from each other. The Duke was just as absorbed as she was.

They went and sat on a sofa, and in low, completely joyous

monotones they talked to each other. No one else existed for them. The rest of us could have been out on the street for all they cared. Time went by. Finally Hervé Mille, a charming man who was one of the six, said, "Coco, I thought we were all invited here to *dine*."

Coco turned from the Duke—the first time—and batted her eyes at the butler, and we proceeded into the dining room. She was on his right at dinner . . . and they started to talk again. Obviously, they had once had a great romantic hour together. Well, I mean, it was clear to the dullest eye. I have never seen such intensity in my life.

The next morning I was sleeping a little late. When I asked the operator "Are there any calls?" she said, *"Oui, Madame la Duchesse de Windsor a téléphoné cinq fois, madame."* She'd been calling since eight o'clock in the morning; you know, she never sleeps at all. When I reached her, she said, "My God, Diana, will we ever see the likes of that dinner again!"

The Duchess wasn't at all disturbed. She couldn't wait to get me on the phone in the morning to have a good talk about it.

When Chanel died—she had never been taken ill; she'd finished her collection two or three weeks before—her secretary approached Susan Train of French *Vogue* with a little black velvet bag and a note that read: *"Pour Mme Vreeland de la part de Mademoiselle."*

In the bag were the pearl earrings Chanel always wore. These were *real*—though she seldom wore real jewels. Actually, on the day she died, as far as we know, her *great* collection of jewels—including the famous Romanov pearls Dmitri had given her—disappeared off the *face of the earth*.

Isn't it curious, though, that she gave these earrings to me? I'd always been *slightly* shy of her. And of course she was at times *impossible*. She had an utterly malicious tongue. Once, apparently, she'd said that I was the most pretentious woman she'd ever met. But that was Coco—she said a lot of things. So many things are said in this world, and in the end it makes no difference. Coco was never a *kind* woman . . . she was a *monstre sacré*. But she was the most interesting person *I've* ever met.

One night Coco was going to stay in New York on her way to Paris from Hawaii. I said, "Would you like to come for dinner on your way through?" She said, "No, no, no. Too strenuous. I'm too tired. I'm too bored! I can't wait to get back to Paris." Then there was a phone call saying, "Mademoiselle would love to come for dinner if she doesn't have to talk." I said there would be only four of us; she didn't even have to come to the table—but I would so love to see her. She didn't come often to this country; I think she came three times in all. In those days the French seldom crossed the Atlantic. I have no idea why the French complain about travel. Of course, they complain about everything . . . including France.

So Coco came with a very charming man, French, she'd been traveling with. She sat exactly where you are, crossed her legs, and started to talk. Dinner was announced; she came to the table; she ate everything in sight. She never stopped talking. In the middle of dinner she asked: "Couldn't we send a message to Helena?"—meaning Helena Rubinstein. Did you ever see any pictures of *her*? Marvelous looking. Polish Jewess of splendor. Splendor! So I telephoned Helena and said, "If you don't mind coming after dinner, we're half through, but Coco wants to see you."

She arrived. It was summer. Coco had on a little white quilted satin tailleur, skirt, below the knee but short, a white ribbon and a gardenia in her hair, and a white lace shirt. I have never seen anybody look as delectable, as adorable. What age was she then? She died at eighty-eight. What difference did it make? Helena Rubinstein was in a very distinguished coat to the ground. By "distinguished" I mean the buttonholes and the loops were so beautiful; the collar was really high; the coat was bright shocking-pink Chinese silk. The two women stood facing each other. Then they went back to Reed's room. After a while I went back to see if they were all right; I thought perhaps they had a suicide pact! They hadn't moved. Helena said, "I only like your husband's room. I love it here." The two of them stayed in there the rest of the evening talking about God knows what. I went in from time to time to check up on them. They never sat down. They stood—like men—and talked for four hours. I'd never been in the presence of such strength of personality. Both of them. Neither of them was a real beauty. They both came from nothing. They both were so much richer than most of the men we talk about today being rich. They'd done it all alone. Of course, there'd been men in their lives who had helped them, but they earned every cent they made. You ask if they were happy. That is not a characteristic of a European. To be contented—that's for the cows. But I think that they *were*, at least when they were in power, at the wheel, and when they were running everything. And they did—these two women ruled empires.

CHAPTER
TWENTY-ONE

How I adored Paris! When I went there in the twenties and thirties, I stayed at this ghastly hotel on the boulevard Haussmann with third-rate Indians in it. They were always strangling women across the court. It struck my maid so much: "Such terrible and vulgar people! Why do we stay here?" *We!* I came because it was inexpensive, and I was spending my money elsewhere.

Lunch was never a big part of the day with me. I'd often have it in my little room upstairs in my hotel, my cheap hotel, to save time, so I could get right back to doing what I wanted to do.

In the evening, in those days, there would be dancing. And the dressing for it! Don't forget, we were beautifully dressed all the time. I mean, we didn't go out with any old thing to Studio 54.

I used to spend my day at fittings. I used to fit my night-gowns. I had three fittings on a nightgown. Can you imagine? People say: What in the world were you doing that for? Because that's the way you *got* a nightgown. Too beautiful, and cost about twelve dollars. You ought to have seen the material. The choice! The different types of crêpe, of satin. The different *weights*. The different colors—*greige*, a combination of grey and beige that you never *see* today. The lace! The way they were put together! It was a whole life. The life of fashion was very strenuous. I'd fit all afternoon—very strenuous. Oh, very strenuous—no question about it. And your shoes. Gloves made to order at Alexandrine. Hats—Reboux. And Suzy.

I don't know how to shop in America. In Paris, if I'm going to see the collection, it's one thing; if I'm there for a fitting, it's another. It's all very efficient; the French are very smart—they're very good business people. Those places are wonderfully run. But in America it's different, Bloomingdale's is the end of shopping because there isn't anyone to wait on you; you just sort of *admire* things. Then you see a man; you think he's a floorwalker: "I'm sorry, lady, I can't help you. I'm like you, I'm just looking for somebody to help *me*." So you go out into the street with tears in your eyes: you've accomplished nothing and you've lost your health!

Or I go into, say, Saks Fifth Avenue, and there on a rack on wheels are two dozen five-thousand-dollar dresses. On a rack! It shocks me. I mean, first of all, to get *through* Saks is quite a performance. You get off the elevator; you're in the wrong department; you turn and get back on the elevator. Then you get off again, past the lingerie, past the cosmetics, and on for miles through the shoe department, and then finally you get to the five-thousand-dollar dresses, dangling there, Oscar de la Rentas, Bill Blass, each next to the others on a rack. Of course, lots of people enjoy the variety. They go home empty-handed. But they've shopped. It's a sport. In Paris it's a serious interval in one's life—perhaps twice a year. It's a pilgrimage.

Going to Paris for the collections always gave me a chance to see Bébé Bérard, who was such a delectable artist. That's one of his sketches over there on the wall. Bébé Bérard, to me, was like someone from the age of Charlemagne. Don't ask me why I say that, but I do. He had the *clearest* eyes in the world. Why this should be so I have no idea.

He was my very best friend in Paris. He was the friend of everybody in Paris with talent. And where he put his hand was like the golden touch. Whether it was in art, in fashion, in the ballet, in the theatre . . . Bérard bridged *every* world.

The sad thing about Bérard is that what the world has in

hand today of his is so little compared to what he produced. So much of what he did was *mise en scène*. But the productions that I saw . . . to me, there's never been any scenery in the world except Bérard's.

Once he did Molière. I can't remember what the play was; *Ecole des femmes*, I believe. It started in a rose garden with rose trees everywhere and underplantings covering the stage and rose trellises up here, and everybody moved within and without these trees and *then* . . . the lights dimmed. As they dimmed, slowly . . . down came a chandelier! And another, then four more, and we were looking into a great drawing room. It sounds so simple. I haven't made it sound like anything. But no one could have done it but Bérard.

Then . . . the way he did *La Folle de Chaillot*! In a cellar this old madwoman is speaking of getting up in the morning, and what she does when she puts on her face and how she sees herself in the mirror and how her *eyes* come to life . . . this mad poetic dreaming . . . the speech, of course, was Giraudoux's; but Bébé's set showed the little cellar room where this poor old thing slept on a pile of rags . . . and it was the *tallest* set you've ever seen in your life. Everything—but *everything*—was rags, rags, *rags* . . . but there was something so beautiful about it. Years later I ran the text in *Vogue*, in which Giraudoux describes the madwoman's morning maquillage. It had all come back to me one morning when I was making up *my* face.

The set, of course, was thrown out when the play closed. Unfortunately, there's no room in the world for used scenery. All you have are the memories. It's like an opium dream that came to an end.

Bébé always used to say to me, "You must come with me and walk through the cemetery, Père Lachaise, and we'll see all our old, old friends." Every name on every stone, of course, is a name we've been brought up with—it's civilization. I'm sure it would have been fascinating. We never went. But often, on Sunday's, we'd go out to an old rundown château not far from the center of Paris. The château was empty, and we used to walk around and look at this wall with all these wonderful animals on it—*stags* and *dogs* and *horses* . . . you'd know this wall if you've ever seen Cocteau's movie of *La Belle et la bête*.

As well as I knew Bébé, I never really knew Jean Cocteau. But I remember an evening with Cocteau in his hotel room right before the war. It was in a funny little hotel on the Right Bank near the rue Cambon on a street you never noticed when you passed it. His room was narrow and very sparse, with an iron bed, but beside it was a low table *very* luxuriously fitted out with the accoutrements of an opium smoker. Cocteau was lying on the bed, wearing a little red and white handkerchief like a brigand wears around his throat, which he kept pulling tighter and tighter. I'd never heard of this before and I've never heard of it since, but I was told it affected his thyroid and stimulated him because of the pressure—true or false, how do I know?

The room was full of smoke, and Cocteau never stopped talking. I don't know how many pipes he'd had by then, but it was a *lot*. And I became so dehydrated I thought my *throat* was going to crack, but he never stopped talking long enough for me to ask for a glass of water. He had Jean Marais kneeling on one side of the bed and another beautiful boy kneeling on the other side, in attendance like baroque archangels . . . but I was a new audience. So he talked and talked and *talked*. Of course, I was fascinated by what he was saying. He talked exquisitely, *fantastically* . . . it was one of those ecstatic, marvelous dreams that come out of a good smoke. I can't tell you a word of what he said.

Finally, at about one-thirty in the morning, I couldn't take it any longer and I left. When I got back to my hotel, I think I drank six bottles of water. Then . . . the next morning, I woke up with a hangover that would have killed a Marine. I felt as if I'd been pushed into the Iron Maiden at Nuremberg—with *knives* going in all around the crown of my head.

Once I told my maid that the most thrilling thing in the world was going to happen any hour now. Mr. Bérard was planning on coming to New York, to America! You know how the French hate to travel—but Bérard was going to come. We didn't know exactly when he would come, or even *if*, really . . . but we'd *hoped*. One day my maid came to me and said, "Madame, I have *seen* Mr. Bérard."

I said, "How could you possibly recognize him? You've never seen him before." "But, madame, he is just as you described him—a little man, a dancer, with pointed shoes, and his face turned toward heaven."

What ecstasy! She summed up everything I felt about him, she had passed him in the street and knew immediately who he was.

CHAPTER
TWENTY-TWO

When I went to Paris for the collections and to see Bérard, I stayed at the Crillon. The Crillon was quite an old-fashioned place when I was there all those years. I always had the feeling of total privacy. I mean that you come in and the place would be solid with people. You take the lift to your own floor, and that's it; you wouldn't know anyone else was in the place. Everyone looks after you beautifully. No one makes a mistake: you're not called at ten minutes to seven, you're called at exactly a quarter to seven. And a certain sort of splendor.

Some hotels are created not so much by splendor as by a great concierge. The Grand Hotel in Rome is attractive to me because of its divine concierge, Buzo. Do you know him? He's the best-looking, the sweetest, the most intensely interested . . . if there's one person on earth, it's *you*. Everybody gets the same treatment. And at the same time he's talking Arabic to somebody in Cairo, and he picks up the next phone and is talking God knows what to somebody in Borneo.

I've come in the middle of the night, I've just telephoned, and he is there and he has a room and everything is hunky-dory. But you wouldn't get that from the French or the English.

Do you know the Cavendish on Jermyn Street in London? Rosa Lewis was the proprietress. She was once the mistress of Edward

VII and was passed on to Lord Ribblesdale, who was painted by John Sargent—the beautiful one with the top hat. He left her this hotel, which was rundown but had great character. She had a somewhat arbitrary system of billing. If she liked you or she knew you were a student and didn't have much money, you could stay at the Cavendish for almost nothing. But if you had a rich name, and especially an American name, she could really sock it to you when the bill arrived.

Dolly Schiff, the daughter of Mortimer Schiff, the banker, and I were in London together—it must have been in '30, '31—and Dolly said: "Let's have lunch at the Cavendish."

I said, "I never heard of anybody *lunching* there. I wonder if they have a dining room."

"Of course they have a dining room."

The doorman, a little short man, came up to us.

We said, "We'd like to have some lunch, a very light lunch."

In a few minutes a little white terrier appeared. And then in another moment Rosa herself appeared. She was an enormous woman; she filled a lot of space. She had a bottle of champagne in her hand. "Now, you young ladies, you're both American, aren't you?" Very, very anxious to know our names. If Dolly says that she's a Schiff, we're just in for it; we'll get the bill for fifty quid to pay for the last hotel guests she charged a few shillings for a week's stay because she liked them.

She got out a card table in her private little sitting room and put down the champagne. There's never been such an attractive lunch, ever. But she kept prying, trying to find out who we were. Finally she said, "Now, how would you like to see some of my pretty rooms?"

"That would be lovely."

Dolly said, "I have a lesson at the Royal School of Needlework"—she really did; it wasn't an excuse at all—"and I mustn't be late for it. So I'll leave you here."

She took my car. I couldn't get out of the hotel. I began to panic. Rosa Lewis took me upstairs. She opened a door. "Major! *Major!* Are you there? *Here's an American girl for you!*" She pushed me in and then kept pushing me into the bathroom where the old boy—

you won't believe it!—was lying in his bath, staring up at me from one of those huge tubs with claw feet.

I said, "I beg your pardon. I guess we all know our hostess: she's very exuberant and very sort of . . . and good afternoon."

And down I went, as fast as I could get there, to *anyplace*. I mean anyplace! Down the back stairs and out into Jermyn Street, where I hailed a cab!

What an adventure!

Did you know I'm always having the most extraordinary conversations with taxicab drivers? They have views, I can tell you, on *everything*. Just the other day I walked out to the corner of Park Avenue, hailed a cab, stepped into it, and asked to be taken to the Museum. It was a Monday and I was back in business, so I took out my papers and stretched my legs, as I always do when I'm alone in a cab. After five blocks or so, the cab stopped at a red light and the driver said, "Madam"—I knew he'd been looking at me in the mirror for the past five blocks—"would you mind if I asked you a question? Do you remember in the middle of the war when I drove you and Clark Gable to the end of Long Island to visit your friend Millicent Rogers?"

"Yes," I said, "I remember it very well. And I remember you, too."

Millicent had picked up this driver during the war. Because of the gas rationing she wasn't allowed a car and driver, but she took a fancy to this man and his taxi, and he practically became a member of the family. She'd send him out with her maid to match a pair of sandals, or if she needed her maid at home, she'd send him out to match this color shirt and this color cardigan. . . . Eventually, he became totally her employee, and anytime the two of us went anywhere, she'd send this taxi for me, and this man. Her one and only beloved taxi driver.

He never looked around at me. He looked through the mirror and we talked about Millicent Rogers the rest of the way to the Museum.

I didn't give him a big tip. That would have been patronizing. But as I left him, I said, "Neither of us will ever forget that beautiful woman, will we?"

Talk about *style*! Millicent and Elsie Mendl were the two women in my "American Women of Style" show at the Museum I knew best. Millicent often lived in St. Anton, in Austria. What was so charming was that she used to go into Innsbruck to sketch all the nineteenth-century costumes in the museum and have them made up by the village tailor. Then she'd arrive in Paris wearing a really nifty black Schiaparelli suit . . . matching this with the shirt that she'd had made in the village and also some marvelous thing on her head. Or else she'd have on a very chic hat and a dirndl skirt.

Have I ever told you about the night I saw Millicent at a party at the old Ritz-Carlton here in New York? She started out the evening wearing a dress by Paquin—black silk with a bustle and a train. When dessert was served, she spilled some ice cream and left the room to change into another dress. When the coffee was served, she spilled some of *that* and went off to change into *another* dress. Millicent's pure American: Standard Oil—that's H. H. Rogers. After divorcing Millicent's mother he went through marriage after marriage to be free, and in a hurry, to marry yet another: one of his ex-wives was dug up because she had glass in her stomach, another because she had gunpowder in her something or other . . . one scandal after another.

Millicent liked beautiful men, and she was just *mad* about Clark Gable. Mad! They were having a big love affair. He wasn't all that handsome. His head was too big. She was seductive beyond discipline . . . a lot for Clark to handle. Perhaps a European could have done it, but he was an American and he was *very* naïve. He was meat and potatoes—and sex. I'm sure he was never terrible to her in the way of cheating on her in a common way, but he *drank*. Clark would order three cases of scotch, lock himself in his hotel room, and give orders that no calls were to be put through. He didn't shave, he didn't bathe—he *drank*. And ten days later, or *two weeks* later, he emerged.

But I wish I could give you a load of his *eyelashes*! He had the most beautiful eyelashes I've ever seen on a man—on a *human being*. They were exactly like a Shetland pony's. Now you're probably not as intimate with Shetland ponies as I am. They're terrible little beasts—but they have the longest, *fuzziest* eyelashes of any creature you've ever seen. Clark's were *exactly* like that.

I remember one evening with him at El Morocco when it was at the height of its chic. We arrived; we stood behind the red velvet rope. By then, the word had gone out that Mr. Gable was in the house, and Mr. John Perona, the owner, came to take us to our table. Clark grabbed my hand. "Don't look left," he said, "and don't look right—just keep walking. Hold on to your hat, kid—the place is gonna *blow!*"

As he *said* it . . . the place went berserk—I mean *berserk!* The stares! The people leaning out over their tables! These are "sophisticated" people I'm talking about . . . it was almost *animalique*, like a roaring zoo. All I can tell you is that that place *did* blow. Power has got to be the most *intoxicating* thing in the world—and of all forms of power, the most intoxicating is *fame*.

"Hold on to your hat, kid. . . ." That's what Clark said. Exactly. I wasn't wearing a hat, as you can imagine. I was wearing what I always wore in the forties—a snood, like a little Goya, shall we say.

CHAPTER
TWENTY-THREE

I think the Hearsts paid me eighteen thousand dollars a year for twenty-eight years for working at *Harper's Bazaar*. San Simeon must have been where the Hearst money went. *I* certainly never saw any of it.

I was the most economical thing that ever happened to the Hearst Corporation. Perhaps they loved me because I never knew how to get any money out of them. They were never known for their largesse. That's why I finally left.

Carmel Snow had been a wonderful editor. She was keen as mustard right up until the time in my last years at *Harper's Bazaar* when she simply stopped coming into the office. I think she could no longer stand the pressures. I think she lost the will. For two or three years she was fading away, and although it never occurred to me that I was running the magazine during those years, that's what I was doing. After twenty-eight years, in 1959, the Hearsts gave me a raise —a thousand dollars. Can you imagine? Would you give your cook that after she'd worked for you for twenty-eight years?

The only person to go to for a raise when I was with *Harper's Bazaar* was Richard Berlin. He ran the empire for old W. R.

Hearst. One night, fifteen years after I had left *Harper's Bazaar*, I was dining with Andy Warhol and some of the boys from the Factory at Pearl's Restaurant. Brigid Berlin, Richard's daughter, came over to the table. She's a bit of all right. Her father was at their table in the center of the restaurant. By this time he was living comfortably but completely in the past. He was still the handsomest thing. He had been a great friend of the Duke of Windsor's in the old days. Marvelously turned out. No one ever tied a tie like that, including the Duke of Windsor. I can remember the Duke saying, "Dick, no one can tie a tie like you."

After Brigid came over to our table, here came Dick. He stood behind my chair and put his arms around my shoulder. He announced to the restaurant in general: "Without this kid"—speaking of me—"we wouldn't have a Hearst press. She runs everything." Then he began shouting: "The most brilliant editor on the block . . ." et cetera, et cetera. He was living completely in the past.

At this point, Brigid interrupted and said, "Well, then, don't forget, you have to give Diana a raise. She wants a raise, Daddy."

And so Daddy said, "Anything she wants, we *give*!!" He seemed to have no idea where he was.

When he was in his prime, the Hearst people had been nowhere near so forthcoming. So when the boys at *Vogue*—Pat Patcevitch and Alex Liberman—came to see me . . . suddenly I made up my mind to listen to them. They wanted me to shift to them. I said, "Listen, I like everything here. I like it where I am. You've got to offer me a lot."

"We're offering you the moon and sixpence," they said—and they did. They offered me a very large salary, an endless expense account . . . and Europe whenever I wanted to go.

That's what hooked me. Carmel Snow had always covered the Paris collections for *Harper's Bazaar*. As much as I'd seen of America, I wanted to get back to Europe. So I moved to the Condé Nast Press and *Vogue*.

I had loved Condé, you know. This terrible thing had defeated him—stock market in '29. Eighteen million, which of course was his personal savings of a lifetime. He died in 1942. Sam Newhouse, whom I adored, told me that he bought *Vogue* for a million dollars from the Condé Nast Press to give to his wife, Mitzi, for Christmas, to see what she could do with it. Condé being dead, there was nobody there with any sort of ink in his blood. No one.

I was given Condé's office when I arrived. I was terribly flattered. His office was enormous. I did the most terrible thing. I said to Patcevitch, "Listen, Pat, I cannot sit at a desk and watch someone walk for that length of time into a room. I can't do it. I feel like saying, 'Hurry up, get going a little faster.' " So I cut off the end of the room—can you imagine?—with a partition. I mean, this was like cutting off part of St. Peter's in Rome.

I made a big secretarial office and put three secretaries in there. I had wonderful English secretaries; they kept everything in perfect order, so when I came in in the morning it looked as if I were very neat. Some people have huge round tables, like dining-room tables, where they can have meetings. Because I never *have* a meeting and never *attend* a meeting and wouldn't know *what to do* with a meeting, I just had a big black desk for myself. Beyond it was a big, long table of the same black lacquer, where the photographs were stacked. I had my bulletin board. I had a leopardskin carpet, I think, and leopardskin upholstery. And scarlet walls. It wasn't at all exotic. I hate exoticism because it's so silly. I had two Swedish cane chairs that were simply beautiful—for guests to sit in—but only two of them. Then a little sofa. And the rest was all bookshelves. It was a very workaday office, no chichi, and lots of space and fresh air. I was there till about half past seven every night. It got awfully trafficky in there. All the London lads were coming over. All the divine girls from Czechoslovakia and Poland . . . and oh, my God, the girls were so good-looking! The photographers were going crazy—some more than others. Do you know the Italian photographer Penati? He sort of floated into our lives like a strange cloud. I had seen in an Italian magazine some photographs he'd taken of the children of royalty, who, of course, are always the most beautiful children in the world. The Italian royalty may not have been *quite* in the beauty department, but then you must remember that the grandmother—I may be a generation or so off—was the daughter of a goatherd. But they're almost always wonderful looking, aren't they? They always seem to be in sailor suits. I took the photographs in to Alex Liberman and said, "This chap is a dream."

An Italian friend told me a marvelous story about Penati. Apparently, everyone in Turin, in Milan, was crazy about his photographs of children. Once, he was asked by a very social Milanese family to photograph their children for a Christmas present for the father of the family.

Penati said, "All right; if you want me to photograph your children, I've got to be totally and completely alone with them."

The family protested. They said, "Somebody must be there. The phone will ring; there will be parcels being dropped off from the market. And, after all, we have to eat."

He said, "No, it's impossible. If people are going to be around, I can't photograph the children."

They said, "Well, you've got to make one exception. We insist that the *governess* stay. We absolutely insist!"

So he said, "All right, I'll come at nine in the morning, and no one else is to come in until five."

So the family and household went out then and spent the day wandering around Milan—they shopped; they went to the zoo. They finally returned about half past five. Quiet. Quiet as anything. They pushed open the door. All the children were sitting on the floor eating huge bowls, like basins, of ice cream, and there were cakes everywhere. And the governess was completely nude on the sofa being photographed by Penati!

Isn't it divine?

Well, you can imagine how *he* felt working for *Vogue* with all these extraordinary beauties pouring in from Europe.

I don't think anyone has ever been in a better place at a better time than I was when I was editor of *Vogue*. *Vogue* always did stand for people's lives. I mean, a new dress doesn't get you anywhere;

it's the life you're living in the dress, and the sort of life you had lived before, and what you will do in it later.

Like all great times, the sixties were about personalities. It was the first time when mannequins *became* personalities. It was a time of great goals, an *inventive* time . . . and these girls invented *themselves.* Naturally, as an editor I was there to help them along.

Twiggy! I didn't discover her—not *actually.* I knew who she was and I sent for her. I'd seen her once in *Elle* in a very, very small picture—just the head. Then this strange, *macabre* little *bit,* like a waif, came to see me in New York with hair like cornsilk, the most wonderful skin and bones . . . and then she'd open her mouth and the most extraordinary English would come out. "Blimey!" she'd say, with the *face* of an English beauty. There's never been a Cockney like Twiggy—but then, the sixties were the great era for Cockneys.

Twiggy was never without a bodyguard. When she came to see me in my office or when we'd be fitting clothes, he'd always be sitting just outside the door with this big loose bag in front of him. His name was Monk, I recall, and we'd talk. One day I said, "What's in the bag? Guns?"

"Yeah," he said, and opened it up. There must have been seventeen of them in there.

"Oooh . . . my word!" I said. "We *are* safe."

Then there was Cher. I didn't invent *her* either—I don't think anyone ever suggested one *thing* to Cher—but it was certainly me who brought her into the world of *Vogue.* I must tell you where I found her—where I *discovered* her.

It was in Morocco on a little strip of beach between Mohammadia and Rabat. Reed and I had gone there to visit my son Frecky's little family. We were staying in a hotel with tiny rooms like monks' cells right next to where one of the king's palaces was being built, and every day our grandsons would visit and we'd go to the beach together. One day, on the beach, a piece of newspaper blew our way. It must have been from a Czechoslovakian paper or something, because I couldn't read the language—I know it wasn't Arabic, which, naturally, I read *fluently*—but on the scrap of newspaper was a picture of this perfectly *marvelous*-looking girl. It was Cher. So I put her picture in my attaché case and took it back to New York with me.

"My God," I said when I got back to *Vogue*, "this girl's a *dream*! I suppose you've already used her—tell me about her."

No one had heard of her, at least not in my office—though they should have. So I tracked her down, sent for her . . . and did we *use* her! She modeled for us *forever*.

At the same time mannequins became personalities in the sixties, personalities became mannequins. It was my idea to use Barbra Streisand as a mannequin. Her success was *overnight*. I sent her to Paris with Dick Avedon to model the collections. We sent her twice. We shot her in profile with that Nefertiti nose of hers . . . the pictures were awfully chic.

What's that terrible phrase one used to hear? "Relate," as in *"relate* to." People were always relating to themselves, and that's where they went wrong. I think part of my success as an editor came from never worrying about a fact, a cause, an atmosphere. It was me—projecting to the public. That was my job. I think I always had a perfectly clear view of what was *possible* for the public. GIVE 'EM WHAT THEY NEVER KNEW THEY WANTED.

At the same time, I've always had an abhorrence of *popularity*. In fashion, you have to be one step ahead of the public. This was never more true than in the sixties. Sometimes I would take too large a step and fall flat.

Once I decided to lay an entire issue of *Vogue* out backward, like a Japanese book, because that's how I thought everyone looked at magazines—I simply *assumed* so. You always see people reading that way, flipping a magazine from back to front. We never published it. It would have been a flop. But the basic *idea* was right.

The management of *Vogue* never bothered me about what I did inside the magazine editorially. But covers I had little control over. When I first arrived, I did the covers for seven or eight months, including one with an Irving Penn picture of a mannequin with a finger on the bridge of her nose and wearing a pair of zebra-striped snake bracelets—and I was told it was a complete failure at the newsstands. I'm not saying that they made it fail to discourage me, but I know, when it come to covers, that they always wanted me to be *popular*.

I never fought it. I remember a man called Mr. Young who was in the getting-it-around-the-country department—"circulation," I think it's called—who had a great effect on me. "You're in the provinces, Mrs. Vreeland," he said, "you're in the small cities, the small towns, the villages and the hamlets. . . . Leave the covers to us. We'll sell it off the newsstands. Inside is your department."

Inside, I once in the sixties ran a picture that couldn't get through the post office in some states. *That* was something. It was a picture from Courrèges's first collection of pants—a top, a bare midriff, and a *belly button* showing. The letters came in. "This is a house where magazines are put out on the coffee table, and now we find it impossible to put *Vogue* there. As the mother of a nineteen-year-old son . . ."

"My God, lady," I thought, "let him go! Send him away! One night in Tangiers! Tunis! *Cairo*! . . ."

"Why did you run a picture like that?" the staff wanted to know.

"Because I'm a reporter," I said. "I know *news* when I see it! What are we talking about, for Christ's sake—pleasing the bourgeoisie of North Dakota? We're talking *fashion*—get with it!"

That picture *was* news at the time. The curious thing is that if you look at it today, it's so square, so respectable—so *dated*.

What these magazines gave was a point of view. Most people haven't got a point of view; they need to have it given to them—and what's more, they expect it from you. I had this most curious thing happen—it must have been about 1966 or '67. I published this big fashion slogan: THIS IS THE YEAR OF DO-IT-YOURSELF. Well, after that slogan appeared, every store in the country telephoned to say, "Look, you have to *tell* people. No one wants to do it themselves—they want direction and to follow a leader!" They were quite right. There was only one issue published with my slogan, but it certainly threw the country. After that, it was back to the more usual slogans: BEWARE OF PEARL GRAY WITH PINK—that sort of thing. And then the next month: PUT APRICOT WITH ORANGE. There's not much serious planning in this sort of thing. It's rather like a woman's mind . . . you sort of feel it at the time. Carry on. Bash on. Keep 'em thinking. Keep 'em asking.

CHAPTER
TWENTY-FOUR

I couldn't take off for a few weeks to see, say, a bit of India. But I could send groups of photographers, editors, and models, and they'd be there the next day. If I wanted to send them to India, they'd be in India; if I wanted to send them to Japan, they'd be in Japan; if I wanted to send them to Tahiti. . . .

Now I've never been to Tahiti, but I bet it's much plainer than people imagine. Gauguin was such a romantic. Perhaps he lived in Tahiti, but he could have made the whole thing up. I'll tell you why I say this. During the romantic years at *Vogue,* I organized a trip to photograph the models surrounded by what was there, and these were the orders: "Never mind the big girls who sit there with one flower in their hair. That you can't photograph, because Gauguin did a good job of painting them already. Our line of country is the most beautiful white horse with a long white tail on a pink beach—no little horse like a Gauguin, but a big romantic horse like the ones they have in a big way in Friesland in Northern *Holland*—all tail and mane. Go *all the way!*"

They always had their orders before they'd leave on these trips. Everyone thinks I'm getting ill natured in my old age, but I was a terror then—just a *terror*. But everyone so beautifully understood. It wasn't what they *might* find, it was what they *had* to find.

And if they couldn't find it, fake it. Fake it. That's a big thing with me. Many years ago I was riding on the Twentieth Century to Chicago. I was just a little girl. On the train was a wonderful entertainer by the name of Frisco. Frisco was black. He had a bowler hat and the most exquisite shoes. He came and sat in the dining car for breakfast and cracked open his newspaper; he looked great. The waiter, who was black, came up to him and said, "Good morning, Mr. Frisco, suh. What will you have this morning?" To which Frisco answered, "Ice cream and applesauce. Make it snappy."

The waiter was very upset; he stood there and said, "You know, suh, this is *breakfast*, suh, and we haven't got any ice cream or any applesauce."

"Okay, *fake it*."

That made a tremendous impression on me. It's the way I've done so many things in my life. I'll say, "Get comfortable, and tap the pillows under you there." You'd say, "There are no pillows." I'll say, "Well, fake it. You know, bundle up with the rugs or something." I'm damned if I remember what the waiter brought him! I was too dazzled at having seen Frisco with his walking stick and his bowler. I remember the crack of his paper, his getting completely submerged in it, the waiter *interrupting* him . . . "Good morning, Mr. Frisco, suh."

Well, Kenneth was the hairdresser on the Tahiti trip. Some of the great men are hairdressers, and he's the greatest of them. So I said to him, "The tail of a Tahitian horse may not be . . . enough. You may have to fake it. It may be too skimpy. Best to take along some synthetic hair." Synthetic hair was better than real hair because you could get as much as you wanted.

So we had a horse's tail made of Dynel for Kenneth to take along just in case. I was in the middle of my Dynel period then— one of the happiest periods of my life, to tell you the truth, because I was *mad* about all the things you could do with Dynel hair. We had the Dynel plaited with bows and bows and *bows*—these big fat taffeta bows, but *rows* of them . . . no Infantas ever had it so good! I was *mad* about what we'd done for our glorious tail. The bows were super, and the hair was thick with a sheen, very long, to the ground, like a train, just like a true horse's tail—sexy, attractive. . . .

So they went to Tahiti, supplied with this Dynel tail, to look for a white horse. Then the pictures came back, and I went to look at them with Babs Simpson, the fashion editor. Now Babs was the most marvelous editor in the way of knowing how to turn the girls out correctly—by "correctly" I mean in the mood in which they were sent—but she's rather a somber girl.

"Well, I hope at least you've got the white horse on the beach," I said.

"There are practically *no* horses," she said. "There's hardly been a horse on the island for a hundred years, let alone a white horse."

"Not *one?*"

"Well, there's one old stallion left."

"Well," I asked, "did they get hold of him?"

It appears they rounded up this ancient stallion at the end of three weeks of looking. He was indeed white, but his tail turned out to be sort of scrappy, and it was up to Kenneth to put the Dynel tail on him. Well, he approached the behind of this stallion, who hadn't ever seen a mare in his life—I mean, he was just about alone on this island, wandering around. Now, apparently, if you go near a certain part of the anatomy of a stallion . . . well, he took off! This old thing, who hadn't been out of a slow, draggy walk in years, let off this wild shriek—you know the way a horse *howls*—and *crashed* off through the mountains. He really took off. He went *all the way*. He was gone for five days.

Here's old Kenneth, terribly embarrassed by what he'd done, which was obviously going a bit too far—in any case, the *horse* took it as going too far. But you must realize, I only take *results*. I've worked all my life on *results*. I didn't give a good goddamn if there were *no* horses in Tahiti—by God, we'd get some there, white ones, and get them outfitted with Dynel tails.

"But," I said to Babs, "look at those pictures. They got him back, didn't they?"

They had. Somehow, he came around. He wore himself out, I suppose, on about seventeen mountains and valleys, *howling* and *screaming* at the *moon* . . . and he came around. They got the tail on. The horse probably came back because for the first time in his life he was getting some attention. And they got the picture, which is too delicious for words. They knew they couldn't come home to me without a picture of a white horse, and, sure enough, they came home with a horse and he was white.

Kenneth has a grand sense of humor. When he got back, he told me that one evening Jan and Mike Cowles happened to arrive in Tahiti. They were going to stay there a month. Mike Cowles, who, as you know, was the president of the Cowles empire, *Look* magazine and so forth, was apparently the most forlorn of creatures; he had been dragged around the entire Pacific. It was not really his intention to go there. Tahiti was not up his alley at *all*. He was there under sufferance. Not Jan, the romantic wife, of course—she was in paradise. A woman. She was seeing *Tahiti*.

So into the bar of the hotel came Kenneth. He went over to Mike Cowles, who knew him, of course, and he said: "Mike, I ought to put my arm around you. I want to thank you so much for asking me to come out here to Tahiti, all this way, to help Jan with her hair while you're both on the island!"

Mike almost fell down thinking he was paying for Kenneth to come all that way to fix his wife's hair. He almost died.

CHAPTER TWENTY-FIVE

At *Vogue* we were always so busy. Ten years, two issues a month, and every article in it signed D.V. I'd read this and then I'd put: "Please cut out that second paragraph, I think it's terrible. Come down and see me about it." And then I'd sign "D.V." "D.V.?" Oh no, I was never called that. Always Mrs. Vreeland. Someone at the Museum, I think, calls me "D.V." I can't think who it is. Rather nice. *Deo volente*—God willing—or *Dominus vobiscum*—God be with you. Popes sign that on their bulls, I believe, the way we write "best wishes" on our letters.

We always seemed to be working on the Christmas issue. I had a bridge table brought in with my lunch on it—a peanut butter and marmalade sandwich. And a shot of scotch. Never took anyone out to lunch. Never, ever. The business lunch destroys the work of the day. It's got to go. I never could have survived going out to lunch.

Besides, food is something I know nothing about. I'm the first to admit it. Reed had a marvelous knowledge of food—he always planned our menus. But though I'm totally ignorant of food, naturally I have my own tastes. I *adore* shepherd's pie. I could eat it forever. I love kedgeree—bubbling, spouting, and sizzling! I love rice pudding and cold birds with fruit. I love new potatoes, with their skins all taut and shiny like Chinese ivories. When it comes to food, I'm really a very simple woman. I like corned beef hash with catsup on it. This is my common side.

I *loathe* native food. This comes as a surprise to some people. For some reason—having to do with aesthetics, I suppose—they expect me to adore raw fish, which I *detest*. There're a few places I've been in the world, like Hong Kong, Japan, and Russia, where my *every* meal has been boiled chicken and rice—*period*. With boiled chicken and rice, you're never wrong—you're always sustained, and it's very good. If ever there's anything native around, it's boiled chicken and rice for *me*.

Chutney is *marvelous*—I'm *mad* about it. To me, it's very imperial. It's very much the empire, Victoria, the maharajahs . . . the great days.

Lettuce is divine, although I'm not sure it's really food.

The consommé at *Maxim's*! That, to me, is *food*. It has *every* bone from *every* animal, *every* vegetable . . . it's the best nourishment in the world. In the seventies I was lunching at Maxim's, sitting there having a wonderful time, when a cockroach appeared on the *flute* of a cream pitcher. *La Cucaracha! La Cucaracha!* The service there, which tends to be quite grand, suddenly became about as fast as you can *get*.

The best meat, the best eggs, the best fruit, and the best vegetables are all found in the markets of Paris. St. Germain was once a boulevard with many places to shop for food, but now it's much more chic than it once was, which I don't like. Now it's filled with boutiques with one willow tree in the window, which I think is so tacky. What *I* like is to look at sixty-five thousand brown eggs.

Toast should be brown and *black*. Asparagus should be sexy and almost fluid. . . .

Alligator pears can never be ripe enough—they should be *black*. What *you* throw in the garbage can, *I* eat!

The best raspberries, too, are the black ones, and they should be *tiny*—the tinier and the *blacker*, the better!

Strawberries should be *very* big and should have *very* long stems attached so that you can pull them out easily. Yvonne, my maid, used to choose them individually for me at Fraser-Morris. Very splendid. God knows what they cost nowadays. Once I asked how much they were—apiece. Yvonne was shocked.

"*Ask,* madame?" she said.

"Listen, Yvonne!" I said. "*Everybody* asks."

"But, *madame . . .*"

"So you mean to tell me, Yvonne," I said, "that you'd walk into Harry Winston's to buy a tiara—and not *ask?* One *asks!*"

It had never occurred to her—although she herself, being French, saves every piece of string that comes into the apartment.

Truth is a *hell* of a big point with me.

Now just the other day my grandson said to me, "I listen to you and you *lie* so much. Take last week, take two weeks ago . . . I don't care *when* you take it . . . you're always telling the *goddamnedest* stories!"

Now I *exaggerate*—always. And, of course, I'm terrible on facts. But a good story . . . some of the *details* . . . are in the imagination. I don't call this lying.

I think there's nothing more unattractive than a true liar. I am a *maniac* about anyone who deliberately tells a lie. These people wither for me. I'm perfectly polite to them, shake their hands, smile at them . . . but to hell with 'em! They can disappear into the *ground* for all I care. Something dies inside of me. And I can spot 'em like *that!* Of course, in business, this can be a rather handy instinct.

But some people *really believe* the lies they tell. They say they spent the day in Albany. Flew up in David Rockefeller's plane. Had lunch with the Governor. And it was quite hot in Albany. And . . . et cetera. They *believe* it all as they speak. It *grows* as they speak.

That was an important lesson Alex Liberman taught me at *Vogue*. We were talking about one very bad liar in the office, who was a very important, old-fashioned, built-into-the-walls-of-*Vogue* kind of person I couldn't do anything about. "Diana," Alec said. "you know plenty of liars," and he named two or three people.

"Oh, I don't call *them* liars," I said. "I call them romantic."

"But don't you see," he said, "it's when they don't believe what they're saying and are only trying to better themselves that you can't stand them. If they *believe* what they're saying—and *you* believe *them*—then you don't mind."

"Right!" I said. "You've got a *point*." I'd never seen it *quite* like that before. A lie to get out of something, or take an advantage for oneself, that's one thing; but a lie to make life more interesting—well, that's entirely different.

Now *social* lies are something else again. I don't mind if you say, "I can't dine tonight because I have a business dinner." That's almost conventional, isn't it?

I once had a marvelous Irish temporary maid whom I was absolutely *impossible* to. I made her tell lies—social lies—on the telephone by the *hour*. "Madam has not returned from lunch. . . ." "Madam is taking a nap and cannot be disturbed. . . ." And if I *really* didn't want to talk to someone: "Madam is out of town."

After six months she finally left me. And as she was walking out the door, she said, "Goodbye, madam. And now I'm going *straight*."

CHAPTER TWENTY-SIX

It amuses me, when I look at magazines today, to see the credit line "Perfume by. . . ." We never did this at *Vogue* or *Harper's Bazaar*. We were very square in those days—believe it or not—and very literal. But I understand the principle. It's the repetition of the name, the name, the *name* . . . it's selling! And scent, although you can't *see* it, is as important to a well-turned-out woman as her makeup, her nail varnish, her pearls. . . .

Chanel No. 5, to me, is still the ideal scent for a woman. She can wear it anywhere, anytime, and everybody—husbands, beaus, taxi drivers—*everybody* loves it. *No one* has gone beyond Chanel No. 5.

Chanel was the first couturier who added scent to the wardrobe of the woman. No designer had ever thought of such a thing. Chanel No. 5 is a totally marvelous product—best bottle, stopper, box—and, of course, still one of the *great* scents. You surely remember: "What do you sleep in, Miss Monroe?"

"Chanel No. 5."

Do you know the story of why it's called "No. 5"? Chanel didn't know what to name it. A number of scents to choose from had arrived at the rue Cambon. Coco called up one of her great Russian friends—a very aristocratic, superior man—and asked him, "Help me to choose. I have a migraine. My head is in quarters. You've *got* to do this. Come over instantly."

He arrived and was taken to the bedroom, where Coco was lying on the bed, barely able to *speak*, she was in such pain.

"Over there is a stack of ten handkerchiefs," she said. "Place them along the mantelpiece. Put a sample of scent on each handkerchief, and when the alcohol's blown off, let me know."

He did this, and she pulled herself off the bed to go over to the mantel; she picked each one up in turn. First one: *"C'est impossible!"* Second: *"Horrible!"* The third: *"Pas encore."* The fourth: *"Non."* Then, suddenly: *"Ça va, ça va!"* It was the fifth handkerchief! With those great instincts she was correct even when she was *practically* unconscious.

The two best men's scents in the world were both made by Rigaud. One was called L'Eau Merveilleux and the other was called Cananga. These were *strong* scents. They reminded me of marvelous Edwardian gentlemen in Paris early in this century. When my sister and I were children, we used to be brought in to curtsy to our parents' friends and to kiss them goodnight, and it was a *pleasure*. Many of the men had whiskers and rather longish hair—this wasn't an American stockbroking group—and they all smelled the same. It had bay rum in it, Florida water . . . it was *clean*. It was a healthy smell—good for the skin, good for the soul . . . and *strong*.

There's a whole school now that says the scent must be faint. This is *ridiculous*. I'm speaking from the experience of a *lifetime*.

I always carry purse scent—that way I'm never without it. Do you notice any scent on me now? Don't come any closer—if you have to *sniff* like a *hound*, it's not enough!

Napoleon's valet, I'm told, every morning, took literally a *whole* bottle of scent, L'Eau Impériale—one of those divine Napoleonic flacons with bees all over it—and poured it *right* down the

Emperor's body. *One* bottle! Now whether it was a pint bottle or a two-pint bottle . . . don't ask me. But this is something I understand *totally*.

You should never put scent on immediately after your bath. That's the biggest mistake going—there's nothing for it to *cling* to. I must admit that Gertie Lawrence, who lived three terraces down from our house in Hanover Terrace when we lived in London—we played tennis together in Regent's Park every morning—used to take a big bottle of Molyneux perfume, *smash* it against the side of her tub . . . and *throw* the contents in the water. Of course, you don't get anything out of a tub with perfume in it—it has no oil in it, only alcohol. This was just a gesture of glory . . . she was madly extravagant.

Now Patou, I remember, when he put Joy on the market, did the most extraordinary thing—he advertised it as the *most* expensive scent *ever* made. Do you want to know something? Those advertisements *made* Joy. After that, *every* woman in America—but *everyone*—had to have Joy. Perfume *is* an extravagance. But it's odd that Americans, who God knows are an extravagant people, have never used scents properly. They buy bottles, but they don't splash it on. Chanel always used to say, keep a bottle in your bag, and *refresh* yourself with it continually.

Even more important, much more important, than scent are your feet. If your feet are correct, you have elegance. If you haven't got the right foot—forget it. I mean, you can have on groundgrippers, if that's your line of country, or you can have a foot problem, but there should be something *absolutely correct* about the foot.

Elegance is everything in a shoe. I can't wear readymades. It couldn't be otherwise—I have a short, fat foot with a high instep like a Spanish dancer's. Therefore, all my shoes have to be made to order.

This is a serious subject with me. At *last* . . . we're on a serious subject. This isn't fashion stuff—this is the *real thing*. I always say, "I hope to God I die in a town with a good tailor, a good shoe-maker, and perhaps someone who's interested in a little *quelque chose d'autre*"—but all I *really* care about is that shoemaker. Everyone should have a shoemaker they go to as seriously as they go to their doctor. I've been very fortunate in that I've always had the best shoemakers in the world.

Budapest used to have wonderful shoemakers. In Paris in the thirties there was a great Italian shoemaker I was mad about—Perugia. His wife was a blonde *so* ravishing—she made Mistinguett kind of musty, if you know what I mean. She was behind a cash register on the rue de la Paix: *"Bonjour, madame"*—you know the type. She was in there so he could keep an eye on her. He made me low-heeled shoes—the kind I still wear—when everyone else was in high heels. I've always thought high heels were the *end*, though they do arch the leg if the leg is sufficiently long.

Dal Co, in Rome, was marvelous to me in the sixties. They had a man there who never looked me in the face. He only looked at my feet. That's how *absorbed* he was in what he was doing.

Then there is my darling Roger Vivier, whom I'd known from before the war when he worked here in New York. The shoes he made after he'd gone out on his own in Paris are the most beautiful shoes I've ever known. In the "Vanity Fair" show at the Museum, I put some of them beside eighteenth-century French shoes—shoes of his made entirely of layers of tulle, shoes of hummingbird feathers, shoes embroidered with tiny black pearls and coral, all with exquisite heels of lacquer—and the level of quality was *identical*. We'd spend four and a half hours adjusting his narrow, built-up heels. And no one ever got a sole as flat—as flat as tongues—as old Roger Vivier. You should come and study my shoes of his one day. It's a lesson in perfection.

These shoes have been awfully good to me. I've been wearing some of them for twenty years—that's how well they're made. Also, I happen to be very light on my feet because of my ballet training. And when it comes to shoes I'm a nut on *maintenance*.

Unshined shoes are the *end* of civilization. It happens that all the men in my life—my father, my husband, my two sons, my two grandsons—have been big shoeshine boys. Reed had shoes of Russian calf, and in London he had our butler polish them for five years or so with cream and rhinoceros horn until they were the *essence* of really "contented" leather. Only *then* did he wear them. I don't know if Russian calf still exists, but don't forget—everything we did in those days was for *forever*. And it was a very normal thing for English gents to use rhinoceros horn on fine leather. Leather is alive and lives as it is kept.

For years Yvonne used the rhinoceros horn on my shoes. A highly emotional French lady, she wouldn't lift a finger to polish the furniture, but she meticulously stained and polished all my shoes after each wearing—including the soles. Why, I wouldn't *dream* of wearing shoes with untreated soles. I mean, you go out to dinner and suddenly you lift your foot and the soles aren't impeccable . . . what could be more ordinary?

And footsteps! I can't stand the vulgarity of a woman who makes a noise when she walks. It's all right for soldiers, but when I was growing up the quintessence of breeding in a lady was a quiet footstep. Well, it is to me still. Do you know that I let a brilliant worker go at *Vogue* because of the way she walked—the *clank* of those heels! She went to live in Paris after I talked to her. I said, "I can't stand your footsteps. I can't!" But, of course, what it was with her was anger; it is a form of anger if you can't control the foot. I promise you, the *heavy tread* is a form of anger. You ought to pull up your instep, tense the leg, perhaps wear a little lower heel. Or else just take the trouble to walk a little more carefully. And if you can't do that, you *have* to go to Paris! As Napoleon said, "Go to Paris and become a woman."

CHAPTER
TWENTY-SEVEN

I don't especially enjoy going out to evenings where someone gets up and performs—or where there's entertainment. I much prefer talk. Good conversation is rare and becoming increasingly so. Nowadays, the custom is to go to a restaurant where it's impossible to get a conversation going in all that din. It's totally wonderful when you can experience an evening at someone's house—a small, intimate gathering—when a good talker takes over and stimulates a good argument. A little restaurant? Nothing more tiresome. Good cooks, jolly fellows —that's what make a dinner.

My favorite dinner partners are the English because they never laugh. I am so spellbound and overcome by the mood they create through their language. Their wit is what is so supreme. A funny person is funny only for so long, but a wit can sit down and go on being spellbinding forever. One is not meant to laugh. One stays quiet and *marvels*. Spontaneously witty talk is without question the most fascinating entertainment there is.

Noel Coward was great at it. Such a marvelous raconteur. "The other day . . ." and everyone at the table would lean forward to listen. It's always dramatic, because all English are actors, and there are very few actors who are not English.

What I'm talking about is general conversation. Country-house stuff. I adore someone who has the attention of the whole table. Too much these days there's this ritual at dinner of talking to the person on your right and then turning to your left. And people are much too keen on even-steven numbers at dinner—"Oh my God, I haven't got anybody for so-and-so." That's ridiculous. Getting the numbers right never made a good dinner.

I don't think men in this country take a social evening seriously enough—that is, they tend to take them for granted and don't arrive with much flair to offer. Perhaps they're too exhausted from the day's work to provide it. It's too bad. Men are more social than women. They enjoy the *divertissement* of an evening, the change of pace from the work of the day. But you can't tell *me* that dining out has become a great art. We might get the gift of it back—if some of the men were English!

Of course, it helps if there's some preposterousness in the air . . . something outrageous or memorable. Greta Garbo always brought a spark that ignited everyone around the table. A great gusher of language. Garbo never called anyone by their first name. "Mrs. *Vreeeelandddd*." Everyone called her "Miss G." Her voice, of course, was beautiful, and seductive. Totally seductive. She adored Reed, and Reed's overcoats. She'd walk up and down our apartment in Reed's overcoats, not to be admired but to enjoy being in them. She'd take one off and then she'd go into his closet and get into another one.

Cole Porter was another who brightened things up *totally* when he was around. Sometimes if Reed and I were invited to dinner he'd make up a little rhyme about us and play it for us on the piano. Nothing serious, of course . . . just as a pleasant surprise for a half minute or so while we were getting ice for the drinks. He owned a house in Paris on the rue Monsieur, one of those rounded eighteenth-century streets which looked as if it had been designed by a swirl of *smoke*, and you'd ring the concierge's bell and the door would swing open and you'd find yourself looking through an orchard of apple trees at the kind of half-timbered house you'd find in Normandy. You'd go in and he'd play this little ditty.

Here's Diana
Sittin' on the pi-ana.

They also had a palazzo in Venice. *Marvelous.* At six in the morning he'd go out with his gondolier and he'd change positions with him— the gondolier would sit in the bow of the gondola in Cole's seat, and Cole would stand in the back, with the big oar, and wearing a little navy pullover, and the little fluttering ribbons in his gondolier's hat, and he would feel the rhythm of the gondola. The gondolier would correct him. Isn't that divine? Everything with him was rhythm. That's why he's so contagious; that's why he never dies.

He was just the most charming man you could ever have around. He looked so appetizing. Such a gentleman, such a *mondaine* chap. A bit of all right. In fact, he was what you'd call a big-time gent. He came from Peru, Indiana. But there was nothing local about him. He had the *patina* of the world. Actually, I'm crazy about Indiana. So many people with style come from Indiana—not that I can give you a long list, but it's true. Cole always had a little patter— sparkling, amusing.

I was staying at the same house party in Long Island when he had that terrible accident with the horse. The horse had reared while crossing an asphalt road, frightened by an approaching automobile, and lost its balance and fell on top of Cole. Crushed both legs. And that was it. It started a whole thing with Cole—survival.

After his accident I think he went through twenty-eight operations over a period of something like thirty years. Reed and I saw a lot of him during his operations. We'd have divine teas at the Harkness Pavilion. He had his own valet. Canapés were served, lovely tea, and a shaker of drinks, all to keep it gay, because he was a merriment boy, of course. Full of it. And then his wife died—Linda Lee of Louisville, Kentucky—a famous beauty and very rich; though he made three times the money, he used to joke with her about it. And then the amputation came.

And then he stopped *speaking.* But he kept on living. He couldn't bear not being with people. He'd ask one or two of his friends up to see him for lunch or dinner in his beautiful apartment at the Waldorf. You'd sit there and talk away at him, and he simply didn't speak. I'd come in, he'd be sitting on the sofa, I'd give him a kiss on the forehead, I'd get my little vodka—this would be at dinner—and then Reed and I would put on the act we'd rehearsed in the cab going to the Waldorf. We'd say, "No one has more beautiful books than Cole—look how beautifully bound they are." Et cetera. Et cetera. Dinner would then be announced, and Reed and I would leave the library and go into the dining room, but we wouldn't sit down. We wouldn't be anywhere near the table; we'd be at the other end of the room examining the beautiful Chinese wallpaper. And I'd say to Reed, "And Saturday afternoon . . . wasn't that the funniest movie you ever saw?!" Cole would be carried in, he couldn't walk, but we would see none of it. When he couldn't walk, he wouldn't talk; but he wouldn't be alone, he couldn't stand it. He'd be placed in his chair and he'd just sit.

One night I thought, I'm going to give this situation a little bit of a push. So I stopped at the drugstore near my office on Fifty-sixth Street. I bought some eyelashes—the longest lashes you ever saw; they were goosefeathers, and you glued them right on the lid with a piece of adhesive. They were about three inches long! They were supposed to be trimmed to whatever length you'd care to have eyelashes. Naturally, I didn't trim them at all. So I walked into Cole's; I got my drink and told him how well he looked, how happy I was to see him. He said nothing, as usual. At dinner, we went through one course, two courses—Reed and I chatting away—and then I said, "You know something, Cole, you haven't mentioned my eyelashes." And he suddenly said, "Well, I can *see* them." It was the *only* sentence he said all night long.

I don't want you to think that I'm being in any way critical of Cole. People were delighted to go, even though they knew they were going to have to go through with this charade. It was difficult, and yet one wanted to say "Bravo, bravo" all the time. At the end I'd say, "We've got to go, my darling Cole. As usual, what a lovely evening you've given us, and *what* a good time."

Cole died in 1964. Reed died two years later. He wasn't ill very long. He was only in the hospital six weeks. One Sunday morning he packed his suitcase with some dressing gowns and went to the hospital to have some tests. I was at my desk at *Vogue*. The doctor called me up. The tests were in. He was on his way to tell Reed.

I said, "What do you take my husband for—an idiot? Don't you think he knows?"

"Have you discussed it with him?"

I said, "Of course not! Why would he and I discuss cancer?"

The doctor said, "Mrs. Vreeland, you're not at all modern. We always tell our patients."

I went to the hospital that evening. Always, Reed had been in the hall to meet me: marvelous foulard, and wonderful this and that. Not this time. He was in bed with his face to the wall. So I said hello.

He didn't answer. So I sat down.

Twenty minutes later he turned, "Well, they've told you and they've told me, so now it's on the table. Nothing to be done about it." I didn't even answer him.

But I don't think of this. I don't think of anything except how wonderful our life was together—the trips around Europe in our wonderful Bugatti and all the wonderful things we saw on those trips, the luxury in which we lived every day until all hours of the night, the perfume, the flowers. . . .

CHAPTER TWENTY-EIGHT

Ah, the plainness of life!

I can remember Jackie Kennedy, right after she moved into the White House, telling me what it looked like. There were no flowers anywhere, there was no place to sit, no one was expected . . . it was awful. It wasn't even like a country club, if you see what I mean—*plain*.

All that changed with the Kennedys. As you know, the White House changed. And the whole country changed. I couldn't believe it happened so quickly, so beautifully—and so easily. How did it happen? Jackie Kennedy put a little style into the White House and into being First Lady of the land, and *suddenly* "good taste" became good taste. Before the Kennedys, "good taste" was never the point of modern America—at all. I'm not talking about manners—standing up when a woman comes into a room. The Kennedys released a positive attitude toward culture, toward style . . . and, since then, we've never gone back.

I had a *small* part in this. I occasionally gave Jackie advice about clothes. I did suggest that she carry a sable muff on Inauguration Day. It was only for practical reasons—I thought she was going to freeze to death. But I also think muffs are romantic because they have to do with *history*.

Reed and I went down to Washington for the Inauguration. We went to the ceremony on a snow plow. It was *so* cold that day, as you'll remember, and the snow was *that* thick—there wasn't a branch that wasn't entirely encrusted with ice. And of course, there wasn't a sound. The monuments of Washington stood out in this *white*, white atmosphere. But what I remember best is the blue of the sky.

Don't forget that a low-*ceilinged* town is quite different from a high-ceilinged city like New York, all cluttered up with bricks and mortar and hideous glass skyscrapers. New York is really quite meager in a snowstorm. But Washington that day was so *clean*. And the dome of the Capitol stood out against this *blue* sky—blue like a China blue. I'll never forget that blue—or that day.

The experience was identical to the impression the coronation of George V had made on me as a child. It didn't have to do with grandeur, of course, but it had to do with something very special. . . . I know too little about America, but that day, for the first time in my life, I felt like an American.

My son Frecky, who really knew the Kennedys better than I did—he and his wife, Betty, knew them from Washington—was with the American Embassy in Rabat when Jack Kennedy was assassinated. He told me that when they woke up that morning—the news had come through to Rabat during the night—the front steps of their house were *absolutely* covered with little bunches of flowers. Then . . . when my two grandsons went to school that morning, every child stood outside and waited for them to go inside first.

The manners of Eastern countries are so refined.

Shortly before the assassination, my friend Whitney Warren had called me from San Francisco. He's a rich connoisseur of beautiful things and has a charming collection of paintings and porcelain and a ravishing house on Telegraph Hill which looks out on Chinatown. His father was a famous architect who had a scandalous affair with Cécile Sorel of the Comédie-Française—their love letters are in the

Bibliothèque Nationale. She was a woman of the great gesture. When her husband ended up in the bankruptcy courts, she left the Comédie-Française for the Casino de Paris to make money. She spent hours, this great actress, learning how to come down the long curved stair-case of the Casino stage, just to walk down at the right speed, with the plumes waving, and the diamonds *in* the plumes, and her arms stretched up, and when she reached the bottom step she called out across the footlights, *"Ai-je bien descendu?"*—Did I come down well?—and the audience went *insane*.

Well, that was Whitney Warren's father's love, and we must not get too far afield or we'll forget where we began. Which was that Whitney Warren called me from San Francisco and said, "I admire Mrs. Kennedy so much that I want to give her the most I can give. I want to give her the Sargent."

I knew the painting *so* well. A few years before, Whitney had loaned us his house on Telegraph Hill for two weeks while he was away in Europe. I had his bedroom, which was built almost like the prow of a ship, with round windows on three sides framing the most extraordinary views. Between the windows was the most *amazing assemblage* of divine paintings and drawings, including Boldini's wonderful sketch of the Duchess of Marlborough with her youngest son, and then . . . on the fourth wall, over the bed, hung the Sargent.

It's a painting of a woman in a yellow-white dress, almost faint banana, lying under a black net. The picture is called *The Mosquito Net*. The painting of the dress is marvelous—the way the fabric is draped and the way the light falls on it. *Then* . . . the ex-pression on the woman's face is the most delectable thing. She's half smiling and half asleep, and you don't know whether she's really worried about mosquitoes or whether the whole thing is a fantasy. That's not the point. The point is the aura the woman gives, and the shadows and the lusciousness and the lightness and the whole allure of it, which is *too* beautiful.

So that day Whitney told me he'd like to give the painting to Mrs. Kennedy. "The thought is wonderful," I said, "and a woman who has given this country such an inspiration of style, of beauty, of everything our civilization stands for certainly deserves it, but Whitney, what a *present*. You're giving your right arm, your right leg, your right eye—it's the most beautiful and, in a way, intimate possession I know of anyone having!"

"That's why I want to give it to her," he said. "That's what I think of her."

So he started the negotiations to give it away. And then, the President was killed just about the time this extraordinary gift arrived. Mrs. Kennedy left the White House.

It totally got to me—the whole *histoire* of this painting. I had a reproduction of it published in *Vogue*. This is the caption we ran with it:

> The romantic mood is a point of view: beyond the ruffles and ribbons and laces—beyond all the familiar tokens—there is a secret world. . . . We look at this Sargent painting and sense, within the crush of black veiling and the pale volumes of satin, some secret laughter, some private delight, some coquetry withheld—that slight holding back that invests charm with mystery and magic; we sense that this moment of languor is only a lull before the simmering gaiety and vitality sweep her off her feet— this giggly, delicious girl is in love with the world around her. *Her* world; she has created it for herself, it is real for herself— and therefore real to us. . . . We believe in it as we believe in Prospero's enchanted isle or in the Forest of Arden . . . or as we believe in the world of Alain-Fournier's *Le Grand Meaulnes*— a world which we know, in fact, to be no larger than a tiny French village—but a world so fully imagined by its author and so deeply realized that it becomes seductively real, vast and borderless: the world of the romantic. . . . It is for you to discover for yourself, within yourself—within the silent, green-cool groves of an inner world where, alone and free, you may dream the *possible* dream: that the wondrous is real, because that is how you feel it to be, that is how you wish it to be . . . and how you wish it into being.

I can't remember how much of this is mine. Usually, I'd write out a few ideas and give them to the caption writer to work in. I know I wasn't responsible for the reference to *The Tempest*—although I approve totally. But I'm sure I suggested Alain-Fournier. I was always trying to get *Le Grand Meaulnes* in.

The painting now hangs in the Green Room on the State Floor of the White House. It has the title *The Mosquito Net* and the donor's name on a little plaque, but of course it doesn't have anything about *why* it was given, or Whitney Warren's feelings about what the Kennedys had done for the country. I'm not sure it didn't arrive the day he was killed. In fact, I'm sure she's never even seen it.

CHAPTER
TWENTY-NINE

I've organized twelve exhibitions at the Metropolitan Museum. Ted Rousseau got me involved with my Metropolitan shows originally. He came to see me four or five times—he was an old friend and an official of the Museum—and he sat right where you are now and argued with me. I'd say, "Ted, I've never been in a museum except as a tourist."

He said, "Well, why don't you change around a bit?"

I was free to do it, certainly. I'd been fired from *Vogue.* They wanted a New Deal there. And they got it.

They were not very good at letting people go. One of the great editors at *Vogue* was Margaret Case. She threw herself out a window because she was eighty, she was out of work, she had no money—and she'd been dismissed in the most terrible way. She lived in this building we're sitting in now. From here she'd walk over to Lexington Avenue in the most awful, terrible weather—storms and so on—and take the bus to Forty-second Street to the Condé Nast offices, where when they decided they didn't want her, no one bothered to speak to her . . . for years.

She had been a great editor. Her gift was Society. She really could smell you out. It was a time when there was a lot of prejudice everywhere. You have no idea. I'll never forget photographing Baby Jane Holzer—the glorious blonde of the sixties, wonderful looking!—in Paris. The early sixties. Can you remember what the world was like then? Even someone as sophisticated as Tatiana Liberman said, "Do you know who she is?" I said, "No, who is she?" "She's *Jewish*, Diana!" "Well," I said, "really, Tatiana, this is a sort of a paper for the people. You know, we've put up the circulation by five hundred thousand in three years because we're touching on everybody, so long as they're exciting and glamorous and fashionable . . . that's our business."

"Well, so long as you know what you're doing."

I thought to myself, "I know exactly what I'm doing."

Margaret Case was part and parcel of this snobbish attitude, but she knew what she was talking about. She came from Ithaca, New York, and the story was that she was part of a dance team. You might ask how Margaret Case, coming out of a provincial environment like that, could become so acute in sniffing out Society. Well, have you ever known a lady's maid? Have you ever known a butler? Try to beat *them*. Not that I'm putting Margaret in the same category. She was a very dignified, good woman. She was very good at fashion. She was Condé Nast's right arm there for a long time. And then they decided to get rid of her. She didn't get the hint. One day she was at her desk, which she'd had for forty or fifty years, and some moving men came and said they had to take the desk away. She said, "But it's my desk. It's got all my things in it."

Well, they took her desk away and dumped everything in it out. Boxes and boxes arrived here at this building. Isn't that awful? Papers, letters, photographs. I couldn't go upstairs to her apartment, I couldn't look.

Very early one morning my maid, Yvonne, came through the court in the back and found her. She'd gone out the window, sixteen floors. She was as neat as a pin. She was in a raincoat fastened to here, a little handkerchief, all the buttons to the very bottom, and a pair of slacks. I mean, she had thought everything out!

Well, I was fired somewhat more courteously, I must admit. When he heard the news, Ted Rousseau of the Metropolitan Museum came to see me. I was terribly fond of Ted. What a marvelous man he was. Raised in Paris. He *was* the Metropolitan. He installed me there in an office in the Costume Institute, which has been in the Met for years—founded by the Lewisohn Stadium people. A really fantastic collection had been donated to start things—shawls, wonderful laces, the clothes of the Directoire, et cetera, et cetera, eighteenth-century dresses . . . it's not only an incredible collection but wonderfully preserved. I took Marie-Hélène de Rothschild there and she said, "Oh, God, Diana, if *my* clothes could be kept like *these!*" Everything, you see, is *breathing* in there; the clothes are behind Venetian blinds in these huge cabinets—the temperature, humidity, and lighting are all carefully controlled.

Balenciaga was the first exhibition. That was the sort of spectacle that the Museum officials expected. But then for the third show we put on one called "Romantic and Glamorous Hollywood Design." Tom Hoving, who was the director then, got on the phone. "In the name of God, Diana, why are we dragging *Hollywood* into the Metropolitan?"

I said, "Tom, I've been looking at French couture for the last forty years, and I can only tell you that I have *never* seen clothes made like these."

It was true. They were unbelievable—the clothes those actresses wore. Of course, I'm talking about the glamorous years of Hollywood designs . . . what Garbo wore as Camille or Mata Hari. The Dietrich dresses in *Angel* . . . the costumes of Vivien Leigh in *Gone With the Wind.*

I went all over the place to find those clothes. I got them out of the honky-tonks in New Orleans and the warehouses where they sell dresses for the Mardi Gras, and throughout the country. Of course, I went out to the studios in California . . . sending word to the costumers that I was interested in that period. Each one said, "Oh, Mrs. Vreeland, we have the *biggest* surprise for you! We have the one and only green curtain dress that Scarlett O'Hara wore in *Gone With the Wind.* We've been saving it for you. Everyone's after it. It's just for you." I always said, "Thank you *very* much, but it's much too nice of you," because I had gone to see Danny Selznick, who had given me the key to his father's closet, in which there was a gigantic safe. "Diana," he said to me, "in there are *all* the clothes from *Gone With the Wind*." And hanging in a neat row were all the beautiful clothes of Vivien Leigh. I must have been shown twenty "originals" in Hollywood, but at last I came away with the true article.

I always remember about *Gone With the Wind* that when Reed and I were staying in Manhasset, Jock Whitney's sister, Joan Payson, sent her chauffeur down with the manuscript of the book. She asked that I read it quickly because the next morning she was going to send the book off to David O. Selznick in Hollywood. That book made the telephone directory look like a pocket handkerchief. I told the chauffeur to explain to Mrs. Payson that I preferred to sleep at night, or at least part of it, and that what had been handed to me would have kept me up for two or three weeks. Actually I can't stand novels—I don't care what happens to people on paper.

One of my favorite Metropolitan exhibitions was "Fashions of the Hapsburg Era: Austria-Hungary." Unfortunately Hungarians don't impress the world anymore—they've never been successful, and success is the only thing the world we live in now understands and remembers.

I'd never been behind the Iron Curtain. I've been to Moscow and Leningrad, but that's not what I'm talking about. I'm talking about the satellite countries like Hungary. And when I went back to Hungary to arrange for the exhibition at the Metropolitan, I was so dismayed that I couldn't *wait* to do my work and pull out. There *were* a few compensations: no high-rises, so they've won a battle *there*. The baroque contours of the eighteenth-century palaces along the Danube remain. The two museums I was taken to were absolutely immaculate and beautifully lit. But the poverty! The lack of anything for anybody to do. What upset me the most were the men. It was March when I was there—chilly and gray—and the men were walking along in rusty overcoats and carrying black bags. What do you suppose they were carrying in those bags? I could never guess. Certainly not work, because I never had the sense that anybody *was* working.

Wills, perhaps. Or a bottle. They all seemed slightly stooped, which is what happens to people if there is nothing toward which they are walking.

But if you could have been in Budapest before the war, you could have learned history, you could have learned *romance* . . . Budapest before the war was the most chic city in Europe.

Budapest! Buda-*pest*! There's Buda and there's Pest, with the Danube running in between. When you smell the Danube, you know you're no longer in the West. It's an undefinable smell that comes from the *East*.

The Danube still smells the same. That was the *only* thing that hadn't changed when I went back to Budapest to get clothes for the Hapsburg show. Now it's a gray city with gray buildings, gray people . . . but the Budapest I remember was the last city of pleasure. It was simply charm and life and violins, and you'd look out a window and see a barefoot gypsy girl leading a bear walking on his hind legs with a ring in his nose, or a beautiful officer in a pale blue jacket with sable cuffs and collar slung over one shoulder. Embroidered boots! The dash of Budapest!

Animals were once a great part of life. They certainly were in Budapest. We'd often have lunch in the zoo among the animals allowed to walk around loose—all sorts of beautiful horned animals and peacocks, cranes, and pelicans. The zoo in Budapest was the most romantic thing you could possibly imagine. Did you know that my favorite movie is *Zoo in Budapest*—with Loretta Young and Gene Raymond. Not many people know there *is* such a movie.

Other days in Hungary we'd drive out to the country just above Budapest, which is like the steppes of Russia, where we saw something we'd seen only in Tunisia. We saw mirages of water, the fata morgana. There we saw cowboys with great wide-brimmed hats.

In the evening we'd go back to the Duna Palato Hotel, where we always stayed. Ah, the total refinement of the Duna Palato! M. Ritz had stayed there with his wife late in the nineteenth century and had decided to copy it. *Every* Ritz hotel, starting with the Ritz on the place Vendôme in Paris, was copied from the Duna Palato, which was *without* question the best and most luxurious hotel in Europe until it got a direct hit during the war.

We dined in the wine gardens about nine o'clock. On the way in you grabbed a tartan blanket—fluffy, woolen—off a tall stack by the door. I took two or three. They were to keep on your lap and to put over your shoulders. Candles were set throughout the gardens, and there were *lots* of waiters, more of them as the evening went on, hovering over you and changing this and that, and *no* suggestion from them that it was time to finish the drinks and move on. And violinists, treating you as if you were someone in a fairy tale.

There were two other extraordinary places in Budapest—the Parisienne Grille, a big ballroom with a royal box to sit in at each of the four corners of the room, quite far up, and dancing below, and you'd sweep down and join in. The other was the Arizona. There was nothing in there that could remind anyone in Budapest of Arizona unless it was that the floor came up, very mechanical, very modern, with a girl on it wearing gray slacks and a wide felt hat and singing "Stormy Weather." Why that reminded the Hungarians of the state of Arizona I haven't the slightest idea. Certainly if you went into a place in Arizona named the Budapest you'd find a dozen or so strolling violinists and waiters in red pantaloons.

The *mud baths* of Budapest! Every morning a woman would come to the Duna Palato with some mud from someplace up the Danube, and I'd sit there all morning, perfectly content, with this lovely mud all over my face and neck. Everyone's face in Budapest was so wonderfully *clean*. Don't forget, this is a city where no one had any money—but everyone was in *love*, everyone was so beautifully *dressed*, everyone had such beautiful *shoes*. . . . The best shoe and boot makers in the world were there—the *very* best—so all the women's feet were wonderfully shod and elegant, like ballet dancers' feet.

And the *men* . . . ah, they were so dashing! And they were still dashing at eighty, because they never tired of pleasure. They had the beauty of age. We often went to the races with the swells of the racing world—I mean the Big-Timers, like the Hungarian equivalent of Lord Derby. Now *this* is interesting: the grand seigneurs in their striped trousers and cutaways and *always* a touch of makeup, under their gray toppers. It was just a matter of a little kohl here, a little black grease there, a little this and a little that . . . I'm talking about the expression of the face being brought out. Apparently, this is a Slavic thing—I think it comes from Rumania—but it was as *comme il faut* as an older woman wearing a lace collar. I never took it as anything extraordinary. I just took it as something one saw when one went to the races in Budapest. This was all part of life in those days.

You can call this a "peacock complex"—I *approve* of that. Show me a dandy and I'll show you a hero, as Baudelaire said. I've never seen dandies like the dandies I saw in Budapest. Very Hungarian thing. And in the nineteenth century it was *more*. When I went back to Budapest, I went *mad* over the nineteenth-century men's uniforms. They're the aristocracy of elegance. It's the leather, it's the placement of the gold embroidery, the small casques with one egret feather; the tasseled boots, the sables. . . . Of course, they're all slightly absurd, because though they were seldom at war they were always in uniform—it was the rule of the Emperor that no man at court could be dressed in anything but the uniform of his own regiment. They have the real absurdity of style.

Those Hungarian men are my heroes. And Elisabeth, Empress of Austria and Queen of Hungary, is one of my heroines. She was born a Wittelsbach, and I can show you a picture of her and a picture of Ludwig when he was young that are *identical*—although they were only first cousins. You couldn't tell the boy from the girl except for the length of the hair. Elisabeth adored her hair, took great care of her hair . . . perhaps you remember the great Winterhalter portrait. She was one of the first modern women. She was one of the first women who did exercises, one of the first who did gymnastics, and one night a week she'd go to bed in special sheets of bath toweling packed in beefsteaks—for her skin. Apparently, she never looked older than thirty—ever.

Now during my search for costumes in Budapest I was shown . . . at first, I didn't understand what I was being shown. My little interpreter and the costume curator were speaking Hungarian and German when a box was brought out. In it was a beautiful little black taffeta blouse with a high neck and a *tiny* waist. It had belonged to Elisabeth. She had very long legs—she wasn't short—and was lithe and slender.

"And this," the curator said, "is the blouse in which the Empress was murdered."

"Oh . . ." I said.

It was as immaculate as my shirt. There was a *tiny* slit where the stiletto had gone in—but other than that there wasn't a mark. It was all corseting, you see. She was so tightly laced that there was no external bleeding of any kind, and that's why neither she nor anyone else knew what had happened. She just kept walking. "Please give me your hand," she said. "I'd like to go back to the boat. . . ."

She kept going while the hemorrhage was taking place—tightly laced within this black taffeta blouse. But she kept walking, kept walking, kept *walking* . . . she got back to the boat and was taken back to Geneva, where she died. You must imagine this. Of course, nowadays you wouldn't have to imagine it. There'd be paparazzi standing around taking pictures of the whole thing.

CHAPTER
THIRTY

In Russia they told me: "We're not a royal country."

I thought of this just the other day. A day doesn't go by when I don't think about Russia. One day I was asked to do an advertisement on the radio for Hide-A-Beds. Rather a commercial job, you might say, but I happen to think that beds are marvelous. At home I have a huge sofa and, *en plus*, a long bed that comes out to here. So I said, "This is what I would like to say for the advertisement: When I was in Pavlovsk, outside of Leningrad—the palace that Catherine the Great built for Paul, her son—I saw Catherine's bed, and it was L-shaped. Now that's rather fascinating—an L-shaped bed. Here's the bed and here's the leg of the L—another very wide bed sticking out of it at right angles. Don't ask me why—I have no *idea*. It was never explained to me. Whether she threw the army in there, took the navy in here . . . but that's the sort of thing that I would like to suggest in the radio advertisement."

They didn't think that would be quite suitable.

"But," I said, "wouldn't people like to have a bed like Catherine the Great of Russia's? She *was* great, as Mae West said . . . in fact that was the name of one of Mae's plays, *Catherine Was Great*. I always believe in giving 'em something!"

The first day I arrived in Russia to collect the clothes for the exhibition at the Metropolitan, I had nothing to do. No one was going to see me until the next day, so I went to Tolstoy's house. It was once well out in the country on the outskirts of Moscow; now it's just a little outside. There was no one else there, and I thought it was the most divine thing in the world. And when I saw these *lilacs*—like great big bunches of grapes—falling over the walls like *bombs* . . . I died.

A child who was obviously the daughter of the caretaker was following me around. Of course, I was *raving*—I was so *excited* by my first day in Russia. I think she understood me. But then she ran away, like all children do, like dogs do—you know, they're terribly fascinated with you for a while, then they lose interest. Then she came back . . . with one rose! From Tolstoy's garden! I took it home, put it in a little cream pitcher, and had it the whole ten days I stayed in Moscow.

We're all exiles from something, but *never* to be able to go back to our country is something we don't know. When I'd been in Russia for only forty-eight hours, I thought to myself: Of all the countries I've known, if it were my country not to be able to come back to *this* one would be the most terrible.

When I found myself walking through Red Square in the middle of the night . . . I felt like a child. It was light right up until about eleven-thirty, but it wasn't sun, it was light, the light behind the sky. I don't think I'd like the midnight sun, actually. What I love is darkness—changing. I loved the golden onion domes and the beautiful skies. I love medieval Russia. Moscow is really my town.

And *then* . . . Leningrad! I arrived there late in March and it was still winter. Everything was black—except for the buildings, of course. The farther north you get, the more love of color you find, and no one has ever loved color more than the Russians. When I got back, a friend of mine said, "So you fell for all that third-rate Italian stuff—Leningrad, that ice-cream town?" Really!

When I arrived in Leningrad, every tree was a thick black line. Then, in *one week* . . . it was spring! It was the most beautiful big city I've ever seen in my life. It was bigger than life. I mean, it only has forty square miles of pink, mauve, lavender, *pistache* green, and pale blue palaces, all of such a nobility, such a *scale* . . . wide, wide avenues and squares . . . nothing but rivers and bridges and sunsets and clean, clear northern air.

I adore *les russes*. I call them that out of habit, because of the Ballets Russes, because of Fokine, because of all the *émigrés* I used to see in London, Paris, Lausanne, and New York. As you know, all *émigrés* speak French.

I saw my friend Iya Abdy not long ago. Her father was a great dramatic actor who was known from one end of Russia to another. One night he was Boris Godunov, the next night he was Ivan the Terrible, and he traveled in caravans with parrots and leopards and cheetahs and tigers. That's how Iya was brought up.

She came to see the Russian show at the Museum. She came alone. She gives the impression of traveling all over the world alone. "Oh, Diana," she said, "did you *hate* Rrrussia?"

She's never lost her Russian accent, which is rather curious considering the number of years she's been out of Russia—well over fifty. But then she doesn't look that different from when I first saw her, which, curiously enough, was in New York. She was exercising five Pekinese outside the Waldorf Towers. She had these huge macaroons of thick blond hair, an enormous black hat, and a big mouth. She was six feet tall. New York, you know, was a small city then—you could see people. And I said to myself, "That must be Lady Abdy."

She's one of my old friends. We never miss each other if we're in the same city. Big cities are all the same—it seems difficult to get in contact with people—but we always find each other. She's still six feet. She hasn't shrunk at all. She still has the presence. She's always made me think of a great golden baroque archangel.

Once she said to me, "Why do you stay so well?" She really wanted me to say in answer, "Oh, but I'm not so well." Then we both could complain. That's very Russian.

So I said, "What do you want me to do—wither away and die?"

She said, "Is hard, no? Is hard to stay alive, don't you think?"

"No," I said, "not really—not if you stay busy, not if you stay interested, not if you keep the discipline, not if you keep the rhythm. . . ."

It was rather touching being with *les russes*.

But I do think any form of rhythm is absolutely essential. I mean, we *are* a physical people, we *do* count on action, mood, and the wit of the body and so on to survive, don't we? Do you know what I think a lot about? Surfing! I do think that surfing would be the most beautiful thing in the world to do. I do really believe that. Oh, I've seen surfers by the hour! In California I used to go down to Malibu Beach; I'd stay until midnight, wrapped up in shawls and helmets and things around my face. Out there, they were all in rubber suits, and I could just catch sight of them on the top of the waves in the light of the moon. I could watch forever! Forever!! And envy them. You know I'm not an envier. I envy no man . . . usually. But I *do* envy their surfing. I think it's because I had such a passion for dancing and had those years in the Russian ballet school. Of course, the surfing didn't hit me till I was what you might call a little older.

Surfing's a bit of all right!

But then, of course, I've got such a thing about water. Have I told you that I think water is God's tranquilizer? Being part Scottish, I think to walk in the rain is just divine. I don't mean to walk around in a heavy downpour—to enjoy a fire doesn't mean the whole *room* has to be in flames—but to be *in* water, to feel it *around* you, to wake up in the morning to know that the skies and the whole world are in this lovely fresh clean condition . . . always was a mania with me. One thing I hold against Americans is that they have no flair for the rain. They seem unsettled by it; it's against them: they take it as an assault, an inconvenience! But rain is so wonderfully cleansing, so refreshing, so calming. . . .

CHAPTER
THIRTY-ONE

I've been with such wonderful young people always—whatever their age. Late in life, people seem to live their years as if it were sort of a timetable. But, you see, I've really been terribly busy. Of course, I don't say I work today like I used to—that's ridiculous to suggest. But I've never taken time off to anticipate, to add up the days, to ask the day of the month, or even my own age. I have wonderful friends of my generation, but I've never made a fetish of it.

I used to love to talk to Mr. Clarence Dillon, who got to be over one hundred. He never remembered me. I'd sit down and take hold of his hand and say, "You and I are best friends, and don't let's think of each other's names because we'll never remember them."

I have a terrible time remembering exactly when my birthday is. Age is totally boring . . . and so many Americans can't get on with it. They're haunted by aging, by getting old. I think it's because of this terrible retirement thing. If you're through with work, what do you do with yourself?

There's an excellent profile in *Interview* in which Jeanne Moreau says: "I shall die very young."

"How young?" they ask her.

"I don't know, maybe seventy, maybe eighty, maybe ninety. But I shall be very young."

But let's suppose I was young and just starting out in New York today. I'd have to work, of course, because to be in New York today is to work. What would I be doing? I'm not at all certain that I wouldn't be in a laboratory somewhere studying medicine.

Modern medical science I find so *absorbing*. So many things have been brought to such a fine point. Penicillin, of course, is the greatest invention I've seen in my *lifetime*. And as for the *pill*, which in the sixties released the whole association between boys and girls . . . well, you've heard me go on about these marvels a thousand times.

My own notions about medicine are actually much more primitive: now, a good massage—*that's* what I believe in! It's all we need. We'd live forever! My dear, it's the ABCs.

I *believe* in backcracking! I'll crack your back—but you have to crack *mine*, too. This is a rather strict rule with me. I practice it with my grandsons all the time.

Stretching! I believe in that totally. I stretch in the tub, I stretch when I'm standing up, I stretch talking on the telephone . . . whenever you're doing anything, if you *can* do something else— stretch! In your spare moments, stand against a door, like your bathroom door, and *press* your spine against it. It pulls *everything* in your body into place. Everybody should do this.

I spend *hours* in my bathroom. All my life I've never gone out before lunch. Except to the dentist. It's important to go early because at that time they're at peace and not rattled and tired. Dealing with a tired dentist is really very tough on you. But usually I spend the morning in the bathroom and I get half my day's work done. This started out as a form of laziness, but now I believe totally in metabolism. Also *thyroids* are very important. At *Vogue* and *Harper's Bazaar,* when I was serious about secretaries, I didn't have one I didn't send to have a thyroid test. "You're a bit *slow*, my girl."

The *liver* is vital—and don't forget the gallbladder! I remember seeing a marvelous friend at dinner here in New York when she'd just gotten off a flight from Japan—and she looked like a *rose*.

"How could anyone look as well as you after such a terrible trip?" I said.

"I'm never, never, *never* ill," she said, "although I used to have these terrible migraines and other problems. One day I went to my village doctor in the country and I told him, 'I have the most terrible job. Every night I have to take these American buyers out on the town, and they want six different kinds of wine, three kinds of brandy. But *I'm* the one who has to sit through this night after night, and my entire liver is being destroyed.' "

The country doctor felt her liver, and it was quite swollen. So he told her the story of a monk who lived near their village who every day washed his face in the cold water of the river that ran through the village. He'd always had these pains and *pains*. And one day, after washing his face, he placed his cold, wet hand *there* on his gallbladder—and the pain went away. So he took to going down to the stream after each meal, taking the cold water, and pressing it in the same place—and the pain and the swelling disappeared! "Take a little sponge," the country doctor told my friend, "soak it in ice water, and *press* it against your gallbladder after every meal."

And that's exactly what my friend always did. I've done it myself when I've had terrible, paralyzing migraines, and I can tell you it *works*. Never lose sight of your gallbladder!

My father, at the Hotel Ritz during the time of Proust—1909, 1910, 1911—was witness to a man who had had hiccups for three weeks. He couldn't eat, naturally, and his bones had started to go . . . he was convulsing himself to death. They didn't know what to do with him. And Olivier, a great gentleman, the very great maître d'hôtel of the Ritz who later became such a friend of mine—he committed suicide when the Germans entered Paris—approached the man with a big beautiful pepper pot and a large piece of very soft linen and said, "Monsieur, I wish to *reverse*. . . ." And with that he *threw* the pepper all over the linen square, which he then placed to the man's nose—an exquisite handkerchief it was—and the man *sneezed* rather than hiccupped . . . reversed, you see, and it was *over*.

One night, not that many years ago, I got a telephone call

from my great friend Walter Moreira-Salles, who was then the Brazilian ambassador to the United States. "Diana," he said—he was to dine with us that night—"I know you always put me on your right, but tonight may it be across from you, as it is easier to leave the table? I feel I'm going to have the hiccups. You see," he went on, "I am someone who has been told that he will *die* of the hiccups."

That night Walter arrived. I placed him opposite me. And, sure enough, he started the hiccups. "Walter," I said, "do as I tell you . . . worship the moon!" Then . . . I taught him *my* cure, which is not so dramatic as M. Olivier's. Whenever you see me doing it, don't think I've gone berserk; it's just that I'm at work curing the hiccups. I call the procedure "worshiping the moon" because that's what it looks like. It's rather an attractive gesture, but it's not at all conspicuous. Let me show it to you. Lift your arm straight up with the glass as if you were toasting the moon, lift your diaphragm . . . swallow, release your diaphragm. Then again, and keep swallowing. Then again. That's all there is to it—but the way it works! "Walter," I said, whispering, "up! Open! Swallow! Up! Open! . . . Salute, salute!"

Walter's own hand:

"Dear Diana, You have saved my life. You have taught me the way. Now I will never have to live in fear again."

I evolved that technique on my own. Worshiping the moon.

I also do a sort of unconscious yoga I made up myself, although I'm told it *is* yoga. Once, at the Golden Door in California, I said to the yoga instructor I'd been to every afternoon, "Now I'm going to show you what *I* do!"

After it was over, he said, "This is absolutely the greatest!" He was *riveted*.

Let me show it to you. Relax your arms and your legs. Close one nostril with your hand . . . and *breathe* in. Release it. Now close the *other* nostril and breathe in . . . are you feeling it in your eyes? What you're getting is circulation in your head. Now I've only done it two times, but I usually do it about twenty times. I often do it sitting in my tub. It makes me feel so relaxed, and it makes the backs of my *eyes* feel so great. I made it up. But one minute can change the *whole body*. It pumps the blood, you see. It's *marvelous*. Everyone should know about it.

I'd like to know why Tiger Balm isn't better known in this country. Tiger Balm isn't drugs—I mean, you're not going to get arrested for buying it. It smells rather like Vicks Vapo-Rub, and it has a similar effect—but it's so much more *effective*.

A few years ago I was awfully concerned about my voice. I thought I'd have forever this awful, false Tallulah Bankhead voice which I absolutely *loathe*. But Tiger Balm cured it! I'm dying to take a jar of it to my doctor. "Oh, my God!" he'll say. "What are we on to *now*?"

"But you've never helped me with my sinuses and my little congestions here and there," I'll say. "Tiger Balm has!"

I've also fallen in love with ginseng tea. It's taken me several years to get on to it, but now I'm *hooked*. I take it every evening when I come home from work. It's so *strengthening*. I feel it in my limbs and in my *face* and in the backs of my *eyes* . . . a *little* stronger.

Tea is very, *very* important. The Orient discovered that thousands of years ago, and the English, having picked it up from the Orient centuries ago, perhaps overdo it a bit. But it's much too much *un*drunk in America. There's nothing healthier than tea!

And don't forget witch hazel! After work, before going out, I often take naps on my bathroom floor with witch hazel pads over my eyes. All I need to do is to pass out for fifteen minutes with my witch hazel pads . . . and I can get up and conquer the world.

And when I *do* go to bed at the end of the day, I never go to bed tired. This was something Reed taught me: you wake up as you go to sleep. Sleep, sleep, sleep . . . this, of course, is what's *most* important. This is why I always say that the best time to leave a party is when the party's just beginning. There's no drink that kills except the drink that you didn't want to take, as the saying goes, and there's no hour that kills except the hour you stayed after you wanted to go home.

CHAPTER
THIRTY-TWO

Excuse me for interrupting you, but you know how sometimes if you don't say something while you're thinking of it, you've lost it forever? I'm thinking of Diane de Poitiers. I think the school of Fontainebleau paintings of her are so divine. Whether she looked like that or not, I don't know, but in the memoirs of the period you read that her skin was fantastic. When she hunted with the King, you know, she wore a mask so that the wind and the ravages of winter didn't touch her. Under a full moon she would go out on a terrace naked for a "moon bath." And she took three cold baths a day—fantastic discipline. But what I'm thinking about right now is the motto she had over her bed. It read: *"Seule."* Naturally, she wasn't *that* alone—she had two kings, after all.

When I think of my childhood, I was always alone. When I think of the war years it was the same . . . and now I'm alone again. But I knew *how* to be alone because I've been *so often* alone. Maybe *that's* the secret of life.

Still, you have to begin somewhere. It's like when I was thrown by the taxi—I didn't tell you about that?

It was three weeks before the "Vanity Fair" exhibition

opened at the Museum. I had just put one foot into the cab, the cab started to go, and I was thrown back on my head and dragged along the ground. The whole time—this is *while* I was being *dragged*—I kept thinking, "You've got three weeks to go before the show opens—you've *got* to be all right." I heard my head hitting the concrete. Damnedest thing to hear your own head bouncing on the curb. And then the driver saw me, stopped the cab, got out, and looked at me on the ground.

"Oh, my God!" he said. "What have I *done!*"

"You started to move," I said, "and I wasn't in the car. Why did you move?"

"I have no idea!"

"Now listen, there *is* a mirror, and you can always look to see if your passenger's managed to get in. But never mind—no bones are broken. No one's hurt. Let's get on with it."

So I finally got in the cab, and the driver said to me, "Lady, I've got to tell you something—this is my first day out in the cab, and you're the first person I've driven in my life."

"You've got to begin somewhere," I said. "Never look back, boy! Never look back . . . except in the mirror to see if the person's in the car!"

I've taken a number of blows in my life, but I think they've all been for the best. Never look back! I refuse to think anything else.

A life like mine has developed in the most fantastic way over the last years. Before that, I had my place, I did my bit, I *really* worked—no three people have ever worked harder, *seriously*—but it was routine. Fashion is always *fantaisie*, it was always unreal to me; but it was routine. Even now that I'm no longer officially in the fashion business . . . I am still in the business of fashion, because it's the only life I've ever known.

Being recognized in the street for my involvement in fashion is truly fantastic. It amazes me every time. I mean, I've been recognized by *cab drivers.* I just can't get over it. I've given this a lot of thought, and I think that it's because fashion must be even stronger than the lure of the stage. I really have come to that conclusion. Fashion must be the most intoxicating *release* from the banality of the world.

When strangers stop me, I have the flair to say, "Of course, of course . . ." and extend my hand. This started about ten years ago. As soon as I started to see less clearly, I lost all my shyness. I was never shy in business, but I always had a terror of meeting people. Now, instead of *suffering* this terrible thing of seeing everyone and everything much too clearly, I hardly see anything.

Andy Warhol came to photograph me the other day. Andy's photographed me hundreds of times . . . and awfully well. He knows what he's doing. He clicks the shutter once and he's done. Then he'll sit with you. When Andy came, he said he'd arrived with an assistant. I hadn't noticed because my eyesight is so poor.

"What do you need an assistant for?" I asked. "Are you like French *Vogue* that you think you need a big entourage?"

"Oh, yes."

"You don't need him. Why don't you ask him to go?"

"You'll like him," Andy said. "He's very good-looking."

"Don't lie to me, Andy."

I asked the assistant, "Are you good-looking?"

No reply. I asked: "Why doesn't he speak?"

"He's Chinese," Andy said. "His name is Ming Vase."

You never know what you're going to get with Andy Warhol.

Of course, on the telephone it's very easy for me since you don't have to see. I simply introduce myself and tell whoever it is exactly why I've called.

That is how I got the Légion d'Honneur. I asked for it. I was told by someone quite reliable that you only get it if you ask for it, so I asked. At the time it hadn't been given out in America for years. De Gaulle stopped giving it outside of France because right after the war it was being given to every waiter in New York who served French brandy. Instead, when I was on *Vogue*, I got the Ordre du Mérite, which is very nice and pretty—it's blue and silver, from the time of Louis XIV, reintroduced by de Gaulle—but it was not the Légion d'Honneur. And that's all I really, really wanted.

I'm crazy about medals and orders. Just after Barbara Hutton married the Laotian, she had his Laotian order of the million elephants and one parasol done over in diamonds and white enamel. Beautiful! It was so elaborate. I was talking about it in the office one afternoon . . . and somehow or another news of my admiration got to the Laotian minister here at the United Nations. He wrote me a charming letter saying, "Mrs. Vreeland, what an honor to have you so interested in our order. Yes indeed, it is a splendid order, and I hope you enjoy looking at *my* order." So he sent his medal to me. I kept it for two days. It was rather shabby, his—a piece of tin with a bit of white paint on it that was chipped. It needed Barbara Hutton's hand. Anyway it dazzled my imagination.

But we all have our dreams. We all want *one* thing. That little red ribbon of the Légion d'Honneur—it was something so associated with my childhood in France, when I used to see men with it in their buttonholes. It's impossible to explain, really, but to me it was France, where I was born and brought up. I can remember the people coming into my parents' house with the little red ribbon— and those were the people I had my eye on. And that's what I wanted all those years.

The French ambassador came up from Washington to the consulate to make the presentation. As he pinned it on me I shouted, "*Enfin, enfin, enfin!*" . . . that night could have happily been the end of my life.

There's so much I still haven't told you. Have I ever told you about my obsession with horses? About the horses that used to come around the corner of Park Avenue and Seventy-ninth Street? I have? About the little toy stall I used to have in my room and about how I used to water my little horses all night long? I *have*? Did I tell you about Josephine Baker and sitting next to her cheetah at the Mirabar? I did? Did I tell you about the zebras lining the driveway at San Simeon? You believed that, didn't you? Did I tell you that Lindbergh flew over Brewster? It could have been someone else, but

who cares—*Fake it*! Did I tell you about the elephants at the coronation. Of course I did. What about hitting Swifty Lazar in the nose?
Well, I never did *that*, you know. Why, it would break my arm! It
would never heal. I usually know when I'm repeating myself—in
other words, the inspirations aren't coming. There's only one thing
in life, and that's the continual renewal of inspiration. Mmm . . . but
as I never seem to know what I'm saying, the chances are I've re-
peated myself *occasionally*.

"In my end is my beginning." Who said that?—Mary,
Queen of Scots, no? Look it up.

But where do you begin? The first thing to do, my love, is to
arrange to be born in Paris. That's how we began our little conversation. After that, everything follows quite naturally.

I'm sure I chose to be born in Paris. I'm sure I chose my
parents. I'm sure I chose to be called Diana. And I'm sure I chose to
have a nurse called Pink. Don't ask me her other names. People
called Pink don't have other names.

LEE COUNTY LIBRARY
107 HAWKINS AVE.
SANFORD, N. C. 27330

A NOTE ON THE TYPE

The text of this book was set on the Linotype in Fairfield, a type face designed by the distinguished American artist and engraver Rudolph Ruzicka (1883–1978). Fairfield displays the sober and sane qualities of a master craftsman whose talent has long been dedicated to clarity.

Rudolph Ruzicka was born in Bohemia and came to America in 1894. He designed and illustrated many books and was the creator of a considerable list of individual prints in a variety of techniques.

Composed by
Maryland Linotype, Inc.,
Baltimore, Maryland

Printed and bound by
Maple Press, Inc.,
York, Pennsylvania

Designed by
Iris Weinstein

LEE COUNTY LIBRARY SYSTEM

3 3262 00089 5612

B   C 1
Vreeland
Vreeland
V. D.

LEE COUNTY LIBRARY
107 HAWKINS AVE.
SANFORD, N. C. 27330

DISCARD